Mysterious

KNOXVILLE

Ghost Stories, Monster Tales, and
Bizarre Incidents from the
"Gateway to the Smokies"

Charles Edwin Price

The Overmountain Press
JOHNSON CITY, TENNESSEE

ISBN: 1-57072-103-3

1 2 3 4 5 6 7 8 9 0

For
Melissa Page

Other books by Charles Edwin Price

Danger Train

The Day They Hung the Elephant

Demon in the Woods

Diggin' Up Bones

Haints, Witches, and Boogers

Haunted Jonesborough

Haunted Tennessee

I'd Rather Have a Talking Frog

The Infamous Bell Witch of Tennessee

Lullaby Aggie of Sweet Potato Cave

More Haunted Tennessee

The Mystery of Ghostly Vera

Something Evil Lurks in the Woods

Contents

A Few Words vii

Introduction. ix

Man, Myths, and Monsters 1

The Mysterious Graveyard. 14

Devil Cats 20

The Ghost(s) of the Baker-Peters House 28

Underground Knoxville 37

The Ghosts of UTK 48

Unhappy Spirits 60

The Haunted Bottle. 66

Things That Go Bump in the Night 71

Knoxville's Haunted Theaters 77

The Quick, the Dead, and the Quickly Dead 83

All the Inglorious Tricksters 91

Bibliography 98

HENRY KNOX
Revolutionary War soldier, George
Washington's secretary of war, and
Knoxville's namesake.

A Few Words

When Charles Edwin Price—"Big Ed" as I think of him because he's as tall as I am dwarfish in stature—asked me to write a preface to his latest book, *Mysterious Knoxville*, I was somewhat taken aback. True, I am a Knoxville native, born and bred, and a partisan of the theory that there ought to be a state or commonwealth called Appalachia, carved out of Tennessee and the mountainous regions of our neighboring states. But Ed is the authority on the folklore of East Tennessee.

What could I add to what he has written?

Soon, though, I was engrossed in his latest book about my hometown of Knoxville, which he refers to as mysterious. Familiarity may or may not breed contempt, but it certainly breeds...familiarity. Many of the stories in *Mysterious Knoxville* surprised me, because in a half century of living here, I had never heard many of the tales.

I knew that the Bijou Theater on Gay Street, Knoxville's main thoroughfare, had once deteriorated from its heyday as a vaudeville theater into a smoke-filled dump with peeling walls and rotting carpet, where grainy black-and-white "art" films were shown. And that the once-proud Lamar House above the Bijou had been turned into what we used to call a "cathouse," in the popular vernacular. Thankfully, the proud old building has now been restored.

I also knew that the Tennessee Theater was built in the 1920s as a palatial movie house with a domed ceiling, shortly after talking films became available. It is still magnificent. What I didn't know about were the ghosts Ed wrote about, the ones wandering through the theaters between dark and deserted aisles. frightening those who met them unawares.

If I had known those stories in my youth, I might not have spent so much time sitting in those movie theaters, eyes glued to the screen, as the likes of Gary Cooper and James Stewart did good deeds and triumphed over evil. Later, of course, in my early teens, I sat with sweaty palms and bated breath at the Tennessee as girls from beach-party movies frolicked in the sand and surf, wearing scandalous bikinis.

On yeah, I did sneak into the art films at the Bijou in my youth, hoping for a lesson in female anatomy.

When I got to the story of the Wampas Cat, Ed had my rapt attention. As a small child, I often heard my father talking about this otherworldly creature. My father's description was a little different than the description given in *Mysterious Knoxville*, which Ed speculates may have been passed down from a Cherokee Indian origin.

My father's version of the Wampas Cat was a creature that was half-dog, half-cat, that could run erect or on all fours. It inhabited the neighborhood where my father grew up (of course) and was generally seen just after dark or right before dawn, when the yellow eyes would pierce the hearts and souls of those unfortunate enough to encounter it. The local Wampas Cat had never been known to attack a human being, but my father always left me with a delicious fear that the creature might one day tire of dogs and cats and turn to children.

Another legend with which I was familiar was the much-told tale of underground limestone caverns, maybe even a complete city under the feet of modern Knoxvillians. It probably ain't so, but it's a novel idea—tunnels where the ghosts of slaves from the days of the Underground Railroad, which did exist in Knoxville, search for peace as they wander aimlessly through the labyrinth.

Folk tales, however, are not scientifically verifiable—and shouldn't be. They are stories passed down from parent to child, embellished along the way, probably originating around a grain of truth. The Wampas Cat, for instance, could have been another animal glimpsed in the dark once upon a time. In the 1970s, bears would still occasionally wander from the Smoky Mountains into Knoxville's city limits. Imagine running into a 300-pound black bear in the moonlight, or coming upon a bobcat tangling with a dog. Then turn your imagination loose.

And enjoy.

David Hunter
August 1999
Knox County, Tennessee

Introduction

January 4, 1999, is a date that Knoxville is not likely to forget. On a playing field in Phoenix, Arizona, 1,800 miles from the shadow of the Smoky Mountains, the underdog Tennessee Vols duked it out with Florida State in the Fiesta Bowl. The Big Orange won the hard-fought contest 23-16, and the Vols became national football champions. Knoxville was engulfed in the clutches of triumphal frenzy, and the party has been raging ever since.

Most cogent human beings would frown on the spectacle of twenty-two grown men grappling a lopsided sphere of rubber and air. But rationality is carelessly tossed out the window as East Tennesseans immerse themselves in the unbridled passion of Vols football. On Saturday afternoons in the fall, Vols fans speed down the highways toward Knoxville, wind-frayed orange flags—firmly attached to their cars—snapping in the breeze. Neyland Stadium resounds with a roar as our boys trot onto the field. Then, for the next several hours, two squads of otherwise moderate young men try to pound each other into the turf.

This is a behavior, however, that is totally in character in a town that has been described, by at least one writer, as a cross between Paris, France, and Dodge City, Kansas. Knoxville has always been a high-spirited town—politically as well as culturally. It is well-steeped in history and firmly welded to the considerable fortunes of East Tennessee.

Knoxville was, at one time, the capital of the Territory South of the Ohio River, as well as the capital of the new state of Tennessee. It was the spot that Governor William Blount selected for the signing of the Treaty of the Holston with the Cherokee Nation. But Knoxville was also the home of inglorious watering holes like Schubert's and Ike's Saloon, and the location of infamous brothels like the LaMarr Hotel.

Both the famous and the infamous have passed through Knoxville at one time or the other—some have even called it home. James White, William Blount, John Sevier, Andrew Jackson, "Parson" Brownlow, Perez Dickinson, Admiral David Farragut, "Big Nose" Kate (paramour of the infamous gunfighter Doc Holliday), Harvey Logan (aka, the western badman "Kid Curry," who once made an unauthorized exit from the Knoxville jail after shooting two Knoxville cops and cracking another over the head with his own nightstick), Pulitzer Prize-winning writer James Agee, feisty Cas Walker (called "the latest in a line of hillbilly politicians"), Jake Butcher, and "Zoo Man"—these, among others, were all vigorous personalities who left an indelible stamp on the town.

Semi-homegrown Caswell Orton "Cas" Walker was a special case. Businessman, politician, and self-described redneck, Walker practiced a peculiar brand of rowdy politics that would have impressed even an old backroom brawler like Andrew Jackson. One night at the city council meeting, for example, Walker tried to deck fellow councilman Jim Cooper after the two had quarreled over the peanut-and-popcorn concession at Chilhowee Park. Although the altercation took place in the 1950s, the incident put some people in mind of the bygone era when Andy Jackson was a territorial judge and kept a loaded pistol on the bench to keep order in his courtroom.

Considering its lusty history (or maybe because of it), Knoxville has more than its share of mysterious lore ranging from haunted places to stories about a mysterious underground city buried beneath Gay Street. All told there are probably more haints, witches, and boogers in Knoxville than the Big Orange has made touchdowns.

Folklore, of course, is not history. While history records the names, dates, places, and events that chronicle a civilization's relentless march to wherever it is headed—be it oblivion (like in the Babylonian empire) or new frontiers of prosperity (like Knoxville)—folklore records the human side of the march. Ghostlore, mythology, and legend spring from man's ravenous desire to explain the unexplainable. Tens of thousands of years ago when a primitive man peered from his cave and blinked in wonder at the myriad of stars in the night sky, he could not possibly have understood the hard science behind spectacle. So he concocted a story that fit neatly within his own nature-based perception of the world around him. The lights, perhaps he surmised, were fireflies resting against the black void of night. Thus the first myth was born.

Since the beginning of time myth has built upon myth and story has built upon story. The endless procession of world civilizations—great and small—has each devised its own repertoire of tales which have mixed with the folklore left over from succeeding civilizations. Appalachian folklore, for instance, is a blend of ancient snippets from Egyptian, Babylonian, Jewish, Greek, and Roman folklore, as well as equal parts belonging to both the Old World and to the Native American.

Roughly defined, folklore is the stories, songs, dances, and traditions of a people. A people is a body of humans connected by a common interest. Knoxville residents are a people simply because they live (and sometimes work) in Knoxville. Their common interest, of course, is the financial and cultural well-being of the city.

No other form of life on Earth has a folklore because no other living thing on this planet is conscious of its own existence. That awareness is the exclusive property of humans. Likewise, while some animals subscribe to a rudimentary social order (like ants), human beings are the only life forms that can claim a bona fide civilization. Grolier defines civilization as "a condition of human society characterized by a high level of cultural and technological achievement and correspondingly complex social and political development." You can't apply that definition to a herd of sheep!

By definition, then, Knoxville, and all of East Tennessee for that matter, can be classified as a civilization unto itself. And, as such, the area has developed a distinctive folklore. This book attempts to chronicle one aspect of that folklore—the mysterious tale.

Like in the majority of the rest of East Tennessee, Knoxville was initially settled mainly by Ulster Scots. John Sevier, a French Huguenot, is the fifth wheel on the wagon that includes the Robertsons, the Whites, and the Shelbys. Therefore, much area folklore is of British origin. In this book, I have written an account of some of the more interesting legends and tales that I have collected in and around Knoxville: stories of haunted graveyards, strange cats, buried cities, spook-ridden theaters, monsters, and what have you. The reader will also find accounts of strange superstitions, bizarre burial rites, and other odd customs. Within you will find Knoxville's best-known ghosts as well as those who are not as well known.

I'm not claiming any truth to these yarns. You, the reader, will have to judge what you choose to believe and what you choose not to believe. But I sincerely hope that you will enjoy reading these stories as much as I have enjoyed collecting them for you.

Charles Edwin Price
Spring 1999

Man, Myths, and Monsters

The wren was a sacred bird to the Cherokee Indians because it once helped them defeat a terrible enemy—a horrible monster whose disgusting, insatiable appetite was said to have nearly depopulated the countryside:

In a cave, high on a mountain, there lived a terrifying beast, a demon with an iron finger. This monster was a changeling, able to take on the form of whomever it wanted. If a wife was away from home, the demon would take the shape of the woman and come to the man. It would lull its victim to sleep and then, with the aid of its iron finger, would extract the unfortunate person's lungs and liver. These it would eat. Then the wound in the victim would heal and the person would wake up and go about his business. However, without these vital organs, the person would soon die.

When the Cherokee realized what was happening to some of their best warriors, they set out to find the monster. Some of them located the demon's cave and immediately held a council of war. They decided to avoid contact with the demon for fear of its infamous iron finger. So they began shooting arrows into the beast. But every time one of the arrows pierced the demon, it would pull the arrow out and throw it back at the Indians. The wound would instantly heal.

This went on for quite some time—the Indians shot the arrows and the demon threw them back. All the time the demon, thinking the one-sided contest was great sport, roared with laughter. In the meantime the Indians were getting frustrated and were ready to give up. Suddenly a little wren flew into a nearby tree and began singing to the Indians. "Shoot the creature in its iron finger," it chirped. "Shoot the creature in its iron finger."

The Indians took aim and arrows began hitting the iron finger. The mood of the monster immediately changed. It roared back at the Cherokee in rage. Finally one of the arrows lodged in the finger and the demon fell down dead. And from that time on the little wren was considered sacred to the Cherokee, and no person was allowed to harm one of them.

Before the coming of the white settler, even before Knoxville was a gleam in James White's eye, East Tennessee was home to one of the greatest Indian nations to ever populate the North American continent. These were a people who were highly intelligent and managed a well-organized society. They fished, hunted, gathered, and farmed. They built permanent towns and villages. They engineered laws on everything from murder to divorce. They practiced an equality (of a kind) among the sexes. And they turned the act of making war into a fine art. This, of course, was the mighty Cherokee Nation. The Cherokee were not an ancient people—the first Native Americans here preceded them by about 25,000 years—but they were the first to establish a real civilization among the peaks of the Great Smoky Mountains.

And they had a folklore as healthy as Paddy's pig!

Nature was their god, and their folklore was as nature-based as their religion. The lion's share of it involved animals. For example in the beginning—at least to hear the Cherokee tell it—God did not create the world in six days. Nor was the world "without form and void." Rather, the surface of the planet had the firmness of tepid oatmeal.

All of the animals crowded together on Galunlati, a small island in the middle of this sticky mess, as they wondered if they would ever be able to live on the Earth. Then someone had the bright idea to send "The Great Buzzard," the father of all buzzards, to flap his oversized wings to dry the Earth. However, the big bird got winded after all that fluttering around, and his wing tips started scraping the surface. They threw up mountain ranges (the Smokies) and gouged out valleys (the great Central Valley). His wing tips touched everything and he was responsible for every geological feature that the Indians came to know so well. The old boy did his job pretty well. By the time he could fly no more and landed on the surface, the earth was rock-solid and The Great Buzzard didn't sink out of sight.

Although they did not have the advantage of prior discovery, the Cherokee believed that the Buzzard's handiwork—land that includes the modern city of Knoxville—was created especially for them. And, being a generous people, the Cherokee were willing to share their holdings—that is, of course, provided no one took advantage of their good nature. When they discovered, however, that the white settlers—whom they had allowed to "borrow" various parcels of real estate to build their cabins and grow their crops—refused to move on when requested to do so, the Cherokee opted for forceful eviction. Bloody battles erupted all over the frontier, and it took years for the whites to vanquish their annoyed landlords.

Even after they won their right to stay, the whites were not interested in coexisting with the Cherokee. In the 1830s, with the help of that old Indian-hater Andrew Jackson, the Cherokee Nation was forcibly removed to the West, a pathetic death-dealing exodus that would be known throughout history as "The Trail of Tears."

Eviction was nothing new—the Cherokee had been displaced before. Originally living near the Great Lakes in the northern part of the United States, the Cherokee found themselves mired in a war with the Iroquois and Delawares. Soundly defeated, the Cherokee migrated south and, sometime in the fourteenth century, found themselves in the shadow of the Smokies. They believed that the mist perpetually shrouding the peaks was smoke from the campfires of the gods. There they settled, became fruitful, and multiplied. By the time Spanish conquistador Hernando de Soto found them in 1540, the Cherokee Nation numbered about 25,000 souls.

The Cherokee had well-developed imaginations, and their religion was steeped in myth—a healthy, active folklore of the supernatural. Spirits were everywhere—in the rivers, the trees, and the rocks. Animals, especially, were thought to have supernatural powers.

In Cherokee legend, for example, there is the story of Little White Deer. He was the spirit chief of all the deer. If a hunter killed a deer and failed to offer up a prayer of thanksgiving, Little White Deer would visit the warrior and inflict him with crippling arthritis.

Then there was Ataga'hi, the magic lake. This was a very special place because humans could not see it. Only the animals knew of its whereabouts and went there because its waters would heal their wounds.

The healing and curative powers of water, in fact, were well-known to the Cherokee. In fact "taking to water" was a daily ritual, performed both in winter and summer. Water cleansed their bodies of all impurities. And the sacred ground where treaties were signed and where a person could go and never find violence, the Long Island of the Holston River, was, of course, surrounded by water.

Water was also the home of monsters. There was, for example, the great fish Dakwa who lived a few hundred yards upstream from where the Tellico River spills into the Little Tennessee. Pity the hapless brave who wandered into Dakwa's territory, especially when this denizen was hungry. The ravenous fish would wolf down both man and canoe.

The Cherokee even had their own versions of witch stories. One such tale, that of "The Ice Man," supposedly took place in the Great Smoky Mountains, just a few miles east of Knoxville:

One summer, when there had been no rain for quite a while, a fire broke out in the mountains and threatened to burn down every tree on the thickly wooded slopes. Everyone was called from the villages to fight the fire—every able-bodied man, woman, and child. Before the fire could be stopped, however, it reached a huge sycamore tree which was located in a broad valley. The fire engulfed the tree and burned it to the ground. But instead of stopping when all the wood was gone, the fire continued to burn down to the roots—and beyond.

As the fire burned deeper and deeper, nothing seemed to be able to stop it. The people were afraid that the fire would continue to burn until it destroyed the entire earth. Finally one of them suggested that The Ice Man, who lived in a house of ice far to the north, might be able to put out the fire. Two of the fastest runners in the nation were dispatched to go to The Ice Man and ask his help.

After a very long and dangerous journey, the runners found the ice house and The Ice Man inside. He was very old, wizened, and had long gray hair that was braided in two plaits. The runners told The Ice Man of the problem and he agreed to help.

He began to unbraid his hair. After he had finished, The Ice Man struck the hair with his hand. Immediately the runners felt a cold wind rush into their faces. The Ice Man struck his hair a second time. This time, a light rain began to fall. The third time The Ice Man struck his hair, a heavy sleet fell from the sky. Then the old man turned to the runners and told them to go back to their people and that he would follow in a short time.

The runners returned to the tree which, by now, was a huge hole in the ground and still burning furiously. They told their people what The Ice Man had done and his promise to help. Even while they were speaking, a strong, cold wind blew down from the north. Then a light rain began to fall. Suddenly an ice-cold sleet fell from the sky (even though it was summer) with such a force that the people scurried for cover.

The sleet fell into the hole. The fire sizzled and the sleet began to melt. The water level rose in the hole until the valley became a lake, the fire still burning beneath. But the people were no longer frightened, because they knew that The Ice Man had helped them and that the water would keep the fire contained. The earth was saved. Some folks say that the lake still exists in a hidden valley deep in the Smokies and that if a person finds it and listens carefully, he can still hear the fire crackling underneath the water.

Both the Cherokee Indians in East Tennessee and Western North Carolina, and the soon-to-be white invaders (and, eventually, conquerors) had a strong tradition of supernatural legends and folklore. Ultimately the two would intermingle, to a lesser extent, with the folklore of other cultures (German, French, Scandinavian, etc.) to create that medley of tales that we have come to know as Appalachian folklore. East Tennessee and Western North Carolina became a "Folklore Belt," with Knoxville as the buckle.

Janice Wason, a friend of mine from Edinburgh, Scotland, told this one day:

Hugh's a classmate but he's older—about thirty or thirty-one. Hugh came from Port Glasgow, down the coast on the Firth of Clyde.

Hugh's wife would come over the moor with her husband in the car. But in this moor it's all single-track roads with sheep gates, which means you have to get out of the car, open the gate, drive the car through, then go back and close the gate. This goes on all the way across.

They got to a gate and Hugh got out of the car to open it. As he opened the door his wife looked up and there was this man—in his twenties or thirties—sitting on the fence. But there was something wrong about him. He looked out of date. Hugh's wife said that he had on one of those army greatcoats—the kind you would wear in World War I or World War II, but it was German style. He was just sitting there.

It was a cold day and Hugh's wife asked her husband to ask the man if he wanted a lift. And Hugh said, "Ask who, what?" And she said, "That guy sitting there at the gate you're just about to open." And he asked, "Where?" Then when she looked again, the man in the coat was gone. There was no one there, but she said there definitely had been a guy sitting at the gate just looking 'round about.

One can logically suppose that a story like the preceding one popped into existence like a sudden thought. And one could also suppose that the stories that we hear so often in and around Knoxville simply made their appearance like a debutante at a coming-out party. Not likely! The elementary truth is that there is a logical reason for the existence of folklore, of any kind, like the previous tale.

Moors are generally desolate, spooky places, even in the daytime. For centuries they were to be avoided because many were reputedly haunted. Even those few people who lived on moors kept their doors locked at night for fear of the supernatural creatures said to roam the grim, broad areas of open land, often high but poorly drained, and dotted with patches of heath and peat bogs. In lonely places like this, the mind was certain to conjure up frightening images—the same thing that occurs when one suddenly finds himself in a large, abandoned house on the proverbial dark and stormy night.

Writers have used British moors for years as settings for their stories, most notably Sir Arthur Conan Doyle in his Sherlock Holmes adventure, *The Hound of the Baskervilles*. So when emigrating Scots first set eyes on the dismal swamps in eastern North Carolina, it was only natural that they adapted their Old World stories to their new surroundings. And when the Scots, again, moved to new territory—this time to the land on the western slope of the rugged Allegheny Mountains—they re-adapted their stories to fit the shrouded woods and deep, mysterious hollows of their new homes. So, with each move, the evil witch who lived on the moor became the evil witch who lived in the depths of the swamp and, in turn, became the evil witch who lived in a hollow so deep that the rays of the sun reach the bottom only a few hours a day. Folklore is firmly tied to historical and cultural events and securely welded to the principle of cause-and-effect.

Sir Isaac Newton's Third Law proclaims, "To every action there is always opposed an equal reaction; or the mutual action of two bodies upon each other are always equal, and directed to contrary parts," (*Principia*, 1687). Sir Isaac might have been explaining the physics of nature, but he could have also been describing the genesis of folklore—history being termed as one "body" and culture being the other "body." If this analogy holds water, then Scottish folklore is the perfect example of the effect of a tangled and violent history.

The Scots and the Cherokee were probably more alike culturally than they would like to admit. Rangy Scots were long on courage and fortitude and short on the ability to tolerate anyone or anything that barred their quest for freedom—including Native Americans who had the audacity to suggest that the settlers had overstayed their welcome and should move on. And, like the Cherokee Indians, the Scots had very active imaginations.

Scottish culture is firmly grounded in the traditions of a people so fierce that by sheer force of will, and with a few primitive weapons, they defeated the greatest conquering horde on earth—the armies of Imperial Rome. In fact the Romans constructed Hadrian's Wall in AD 121 as a permanent northern boundary on the frontier in Britain. The wall was not an actual line of defense, but rather was a barrier to large-scale, swift movement by hostile forces. It also served as a screen behind which Roman troops could maneuver. Perhaps Rome could hold the Scots (or Picts, as they called them) at bay, but they could never quell them.

Imperial Romans were the first to attempt to subjugate the Scots, but they wouldn't be the last. Scotland's worst enemy was its neighbor to the south—England.

The years between the reigns of Henry VIII and George II were rife with political and religious turmoil which raged between England and her northern neighbor. The trouble began when Henry broke with the Roman Catholic Church and all England became Protestant.

Henry's chief minister, Thomas Cromwell, proposed that England disengage itself from the Papacy so that the Archbishop of Canterbury, the highest officer in the newly organized English church, could grant a divorce between Henry and his present queen, Catherine of Aragon. Legislation to this effect was forced by Henry upon Parliament, and in 1533, the king was free to marry his paramour Anne Boleyn.

With the Anglican Church firmly established as the official church of England, the crown could tolerate no other. To do so would weaken the already shaky foundation on which the church was laid. But in nearby Scotland, Catholicism held fast in the face of various reformers. The country was split, and Rome was taking advantage of the division to make sure that the Papacy was not thrown out of that country, too. But Rome didn't reckon with the stubbornness of the Scotsman with a cause, and the Church's inflexibility eventually led to its downfall there, too.

To begin with, Scottish reformer George Wishart was burned at the stake at St. Andrews castle in 1546 by the followers of Cardinal David Beaton, a faithful Roman Catholic cleric who had condemned Wishart to death. In retaliation Wishart's Protestant followers quickly dispatched the cardinal. Then they barricaded themselves in St. Andrews.

Among the rebels was thirty-two-year-old John Knox (not the namesake of Knoxville, by the way), who impressed his fellow dissidents with his pious zeal and impassioned preaching. When Scottish and French Roman Catholics overran the castle the following year, Knox was condemned to serve on French galleys for the rest of his life. Fortunately he was released a year and a half later.

Knox went to England to serve as pastor to several English churches as well as a chaplain to Edward VI. However, when the Catholic Mary I succeeded to the throne, Knox, suddenly a marked man, fled to the Continent. There he met protestant reformer John Calvin, who greatly influenced the young preacher with his doctrine of predestination. (Salvation or damnation is determined by God alone, and not dependent on worth or merit on the person's part.)

While in Switzerland, Knox published *The First Blast of the Trumpet Against the Monstrous Regiment of Women*, a notorious missive directed at Catholic female monarchs in general and England's Mary I and Mary, Queen of Scots, in particular. However, the next monarch, Elizabeth I, although a Protestant, took Knox's quarrel with women in power as a personal affront and made it quite clear that the preacher was unwelcome in her realm. Knox did, however, manage to return to Scotland, where Protestants and Catholics were still at each other's throats.

Elizabeth had no use for Knox as a person, but she had no

problem helping him and his fellow countrymen in their ecclesiastical struggle with the hated pope. The situation became confused when Elizabeth died and James IV of Scotland became James I of England. Scotland and England were now under one monarch and, supposedly, under one church—The Church of England.

United under a single crown, the Scottish Presbyterians resisted the efforts of Charles I to impose episcopacy in Scotland and allied themselves with the English parliamentarians against Charles in the first English Civil War (1642-46). They subsequently supported the royalist cause, however, until defeated by Oliver Cromwell and his Puritans in 1651.

After the Restoration, the problems between Scotland and England intensified. James II succeeded to the throne after the death of his brother, Charles II. His attempts to reestablish the Roman Church and oust the Church of England caused widespread fear of the return of Roman Catholic tyranny to the island nation. To combat the threat, the nobles offered the throne to James's daughter, Mary, and her husband, William of Orange.

Shortly thereafter, William landed in England. James II fled to France, where an angry King Louis XIV proclaimed young James Francis Edward Stuart (known later as the "Old Pretender") the rightful successor to his father. The situation became even more complicated when, during the reign of Queen Anne, Scotland, England, and Wales were united in 1707 to form the kingdom of Great Britain.

Nearly forty years later, encouraged by Louis XV, Charles Edward Stuart, the only son of James and his second wife, Mary Beatrice, invaded the British Isles from France in an attempt to regain his throne from the House of Hanover. After landing in the Hebrides and hoisting his father's standard, the "Young Pretender"—or "Bonnie Prince Charlie," as he was called—raised an army of Scots and prepared to march on England to overthrow King George II and the House of Hanover. Exhilarated by victory after winning the Battle at Prestonpans, Stuart advanced south toward Derby but was forced to retreat. The Duke of Cumberland defeated the

Young Pretender and his Jacobites in 1746 at Culloden Moor where Charles's 7,000 ragged soldiers faced Cumberland's 8,800 men, including 500 Hessians.

In the final analysis it was not the size of Cumberland's force that defeated the Young Pretender. It was the Duke's superior artillery, rapidly firing rounds of murderous grape shot that cut the Scots to pieces. The unexpected barrage took the Scots by surprise. They panicked and retreated from the field in wild flight.

After the scattering of the clans at Culloden, the Highlanders were made the object of much persecution by England, who considered all Scots—be they Protestant or Catholic—as enemies of Britain. Some Scots escaped and made their way to the shores of the New World. Many of them ended up in North Carolina, settling along the banks of the Cape Fear River. The Battle of Culloden marked the beginning of the great Scottish migration of the eighteenth century to America.

In many ways, the situation was no better for the Scots in the New World, which, after all, was a British colony. Trouble with colonial governors forced the Scots to move westward, first to the foothills of the Appalachian Mountains and finally over the mountains themselves to the westward slope. Foremost of these early pioneers was James Robertson, who had been branded a troublemaker in North Carolina. Others followed, settling towns like Trade, Jonesborough, and Knoxville. And along with their families, their belongings, and their livestock, they also brought their folklore.

Protestants are more superstitious than Catholics and are more likely to believe in devils and other dwellers of the netherworld, as well as in an actual personification of evil. When the Scots cast off Rome in favor of John Knox, they also conceived definite beliefs in witches, ghosts, and demons. In many ways their canon of supernatural convictions fit exactly with the notions entertained by the Cherokee.

Tales of Scottish ghosts and goblins and witches began to intertwine with Cherokee tales of giant fish, ice men, and water spirits. With each retelling, the boundary between European/Native American lore blurred. Today, thanks especially to Native American folklorists who trace the roots of various folktales, hybrid tales are beginning to be unraveled and assigned their proper historical place. Every story in this book can be traced back to its root source, whether it be ghosts who wail in the middle of the night, underground kingdoms, or tales of witches and their cats. It's all a matter of possessing the skill of a brain surgeon coupled with the patience of Job. Take, for example, the story of the beast with the iron finger. I ran across another story in my travels, a "Jack Tale" that is remarkably similar to the Cherokee tale:

A cave along the banks of the Tennessee River was the home of a horrible monster that ventured forth in the dark of night to attack nearby settlements. The creature was big and ugly, with a voracious appetite for human flesh. It was also said to be able to change its shape into anything it chose—even a human being.

Nearby settlers had no idea about how to destroy this monster. One of the families, who had a son named Jack, was especially hard hit by the creature. One day young Jack decided that he would go to the cave and confront the monster himself.

Before his family awakened one morning, Jack armed himself with his father's rifle and took a supply of powder and ball. Then he crept out of the cabin. An hour later he arrived at the cave. From the heavy breathing he heard coming from the entrance, he knew that the monster was inside. He carefully loaded his musket and aimed at the dark cave entrance. "Come out!" he shouted into the blackness. He heard a low growl. Then silence.

"I said, *come out!*" Jack ordered.

Then from the darkness of the cave there emerged the most beautiful girl that Jack had ever seen. She was tall and willowy, with long blonde hair and eyes as blue as the sky. She was clad in white and there was a wreath of wildflowers perched on top of her head. Her beauty took Jack's breath away. He lowered his musket.

The girl walked toward him. Jack raised his rifle. The girl stopped. "You wouldn't shoot me, would you, Jack?" she asked in an almost musical voice. She raised her arms as if to embrace him. "Come here to me," she cooed.

Jack was a handsome young man and nearing the age of marriage but had not yet settled on a wife. Most of the girls at the settlement were interested in him, but he considered most of them rather homely. This girl, however, was something else. Never before had he seen such a vision of loveliness. Her face was smooth and not careworn like the others. Her hands were soft and not roughened by the hard work of grinding corn or hoeing the garden.

As the girl approached, arms outstretched to hold him, Jack felt as if he were hypnotized. All that he could see was her beauty. He felt himself drawn toward her. He....

Suddenly he snapped back to reality as he noticed the tips of her ears sticking through her blonde hair. They were clearly pointed. He raised his musket and fired. An ear-shattering blast filled the forest, then a scream.

The blue powder smoke cleared, and on the ground in front of him sprawled the monster—stone dead of a single musket ball in the brain.

The Mysterious Graveyard

Suppose they built a graveyard and nobody was buried in it? Even worse, suppose someone built a graveyard, people were buried, then they all disappeared? And suppose, for good measure, that strange apparitions flitted around the same graveyard in the dead of night and you were actually "privileged" to see one of them? What then? The thought is probably enough to raise a healthy crop of goose bumps! Some insist that the old Presbyterian cemetery in the heart of Knoxville is as void of bodies as fleas in dog dip. And since so many of Knoxville's legends seem to lie underground, it is not surprising that a legend like this should surface too.

There is a second tale connected with this particular graveyard—the ghostly legend of a black shadow that floats among the ancient headstones on dark, moonless nights. Is it a ghost or hallucination? Your guess is as good as mine. But there are those who actually claim to have seen it.

THE LIGHT'S NOT ON, BUT IS ANYONE HOME?
One of the most persistent legends concerning the First Presbyterian graveyard is that no one is actually buried beneath the ancient head-stones.

The graveyard, believe it or not, began as a lowly turnip patch. It was cleared and planted by none other than James White, the founder of Knoxville. White and three companions from Iredell County, North Carolina, arrived at the junction of the French Broad and Holston rivers in 1785. They took one look at the surrounding countryside and decided at once that they had found their Utopia. But they also found isolation—not a Food Lion in sight. When they returned to North Carolina to prepare to move their families to their discovery, they knew that whatever tools they would need for survival would have to be packed back across the mountains, including enough food to last until the first crop was harvested.

White, of course, was mistaken. The country he had chosen as his new home was only semi-devoid of residents. Aside from the Indians (most of the Cherokee towns were barely twenty-five miles away), there was the new town of Jonesborough just to the north. Furthermore, East Tennessee icon John Sevier and his family were already living on the Holston River in Washington County, and Jacob Brown had established a flourishing trading post on the Nolichucky River. In fact, most of the famous (and infamous) early settlers of Tennessee were in place.

At the time, of course, Tennessee was still a part of North Carolina. North Carolina, unable to manage its western sections, offered to cede that parcel of real estate to the United States. This move displeased Sevier and his cronies, who retaliated by attempting to form their own state, calling it Franklin after the publisher of *Poor Richard's Almanac*. Sevier not only was a soldier and settler, he was also a land speculator. The creation of the State of Franklin would serve his own interests as well as those of the rest of the settlers.

James White agreed with Sevier's concept, and after living at the junction of the French Broad and Holston rivers for only a year, he agreed to serve as a delegate to the proposed state's constitutional convention. Then he moved his family to what is now the city of Knoxville.

In those days a ready crop was the turnip. When White

found a suitable spot to make his home, and after he had erected a half-camp (lean-to) to shelter his family from wind and weather, the first thing that he did was to clear a small piece of land for a turnip patch. Later, after Charles McClung of Philadelphia laid out the town of Knoxville (he, incidentally, also laid claim to White's eldest daughter), James White, good Scottish Presbyterian that he was, donated his turnip patch to the First Presbyterian Church. In its churchyard was installed the first cemetery in Knoxville.

Over the years the crème de la crème of Knoxville history were buried in that old cemetery—James White, Hugh Lawson White, and William and Mary Blount, to name a few. Today the graveyard's old-fashioned headstones stand under resplendent shade trees, and even in the bright light of day, their cool shade lends an aura of mystery to the place. No disrespect intended, but the current graveyard presents a tableau more like a horror movie than a garden of rest. And maybe that is why there is so much folklore associated with this Knoxville landmark. After all, don't all haunted houses have to be ancient looking? Why not graveyards?

Rumor has it that there is no one actually buried in the First Presbyterian Church graveyard. All of those famous personages are actually somewhere else—no one knows where. Jack Neely, writing in the *Knoxville Metro Pulse*, said that the rumor might have gotten started when the present church structure was built in 1901. Of course the building was much larger than its predecessor, and supposedly its extra spread took out part of the old graveyard. The graves were removed and the resultant jumble of stones prompted a more esthetic rearrangement. This shuffling was completed in the early 1940s. Neely continued to say that none of these events could be either proved or disproved. Likewise, he wrote, the original graveyard might have actually been south of the church. However, he pointed out that the graveyard's present location can be found on the earliest maps of the town, and its present location was also acknowledged by visitors to the town as early as 1790. The only way that this mystery can be cleared is to dig up the old graveyard and

THE FIRST PRESBYTERIAN CHURCH IN 1903
The First Presbyterian Church in downtown Knoxville was rebuilt in 1901 to make room for an expanding congregation. In the process, the building is said to have taken out part of the original graveyard. This led to some speculation as to the present location of the remains of some early Knoxville settlers.

check on the present population. That, of course, is out of the question.

An even deeper mystery surrounding the graveyard is the mysterious, hooded black figure often seen moving among the tombstones at night. The figure certainly does not belong to a living person. It appears and disappears at will. Sometimes, stones in the background can be seen through the figure. There is no sound, not even a rustle. And the creature has no face.

The ghost of the First Presbyterian Church graveyard is well-known to Knoxville youth. I talked to one young man, now a student at the University of Tennessee, who claims to have seen the specter when he was still in high school:

"One Halloween night me and a couple of my friends decided to drive downtown and see the ghost for ourselves," he told me. "We had heard from others about seeing it and figured that, if it was going to show up at all, it would be on Halloween night.

"About four or five of us went down there and expected to

be alone. But when we got there, about a dozen or so kids were already lined up on the sidewalk opposite the church, apparently waiting to see the ghost, too. With so many people around, I doubted whether the spook would even show up. I know that if I was a ghost, I'd wait until I was alone.

"In this bunch of waiting students were a couple of really cute girls—real lookers. Even if we didn't spot a ghost, the evening wouldn't be a total loss. We introduced ourselves and were talking about something or other when one of the girls shuddered.

"'What's wrong?' I asked.

"'Over t-there,' she stammered, pointing toward the old graveyard.

"Well, I looked and could not believe my eyes. There in the middle of the cemetery, next to four bone-white stones sitting in a row, was a black figure. It looked like it was floating around over the graves. Everyone is just about breathless when—wouldn't you know it—up drives a police car and stops by the curb.

"'What are you kids doing out here this time of night?' the officer shouts out.

"'We're watching a ghost in the graveyard,' one young man shouts back.

"Police cars have this big, bright floodlight on them, and this cop turns it on and shines it over at the tombstones. And, of course, the ghost isn't there anymore. He turns off the light.

"'Listen, you kids,' he says, clearly trying to be patient. 'There ain't no ghost over there and you shouldn't be running around downtown at this hour. Now let's clear the streets.'

"'Well, at least we got to see a ghost,' one of the cute girls we were with muttered under her breath. 'Those cops wouldn't know a ghost if they tripped over it.'

"So that was the end of our ghostly adventure in downtown Knoxville. My friend, however, was right. We really did see a ghost. The next Halloween I went down to the graveyard to see it again, but there was a prowl car parked next to the curb. I guess the police didn't want any loitering this year.

"I never did see the ghost again, but I saw it that one time—I know that I did. And there were plenty of other witnesses, too. We all saw it. That graveyard is haunted—that's for sure!"

Although I was unable to locate anyone else who actually saw the ghost in the old Presbyterian graveyard, I heard from a number of people who have stood on the street and peered over at the old tombstones, hoping to see it. The Knoxville police, of course, have no comment on the matter. It is very clear, however, that they are plainly against people lurking downtown in the middle of the night waiting for something to appear.

So who is this mysterious and dark figure that flits among the graves? Could it be the ghost of someone whose body was removed from its place in the cemetery and the spirit is simply trying to relocate its body? It does appear to be searching for something. If not its body, then what?

As far as I'm concerned the business of the dark figure can remain a mystery, because if I ever see it I'll be doggoned if I'm going to ask what it's doing there!

Photo by the Author

DANCE MACABRE
Peaceful and serene during the daytime, the historic First Presbyterian Church graveyard in downtown Knoxville is said to provide a stage for a cavorting black-cloaked phantom who performs a dance macabre late at night.

Devil Cats

Cats—comfort or bane, pleasure or pestilence, natural or supernatural? These mysterious creatures have always drawn out strong feelings in people. Folks are either cat lovers or cat haters—seldom is there a middle ground. Some love cats no matter what they do (or don't do, as is most often the case), while some take their malice to the extreme. One person told me, in fact, that cats are nothing more than the "devil's own handmaiden" and that he "shoots them whenever possible"!

Perhaps one reason for the hostility is that cats are so independent. Unlike dogs, cats do not practice, nor do they even understand, the concept of subservience. They don't seem to care whether you like them or not and do little or nothing to ingratiate themselves. Cats do not fetch slippers or the morning paper; cats do not come running to greet you when you arrive home from work; cats do not have sad eyes that melt your heart; you cannot train cats to play fetch (if, indeed, you can train them to do anything at all except to use the kitty pan); cats have no conception of a work ethic. Cats are cold, calculating, selfish, and indifferent. You either take them or leave them—it's just that simple. (I choose to take them, but I'm a writer and most scribes are a little weird anyway!)

For some people, the mere sight of a cat makes the skin crawl. One elderly Knoxville woman told me that her aversion to cats began under the most macabre of circumstances.

"I still get the shudders when I think about it," she said. "My grandmother had just died. This was in the days when they laid the body out in the house for viewing. My parents had put her on a bed on the second floor. People would go up a few at a time to pay their last respects.

"My grandmother had this cat, a big old yellow-and-gray thing that wouldn't associate with anybody, not even the old woman when she was alive. I don't know why she kept it except that it was probably a pretty good mouser.

"I was about four years old at the time, and although I loved my grandmother very much, I was afraid of actually seeing a dead body. Finally my mother talked me into going up to the room to say a final farewell.

"There were a lot of people in the kitchen downstairs, but on the second floor it was as quiet as a tomb. Grandma was in a room at the far end of a dark hallway. I clung to my mother's skirts all the way down that hall. Then we got to the door. I heard my mother gasp as she looked inside the room. There was my grandmother all laid out, dressed in her Sunday best. And crouched on her chest, with its nose no more than a couple of inches away from her face, was the cat—not moving a muscle and poised as if ready to strike. When it saw my mother it jumped off my grandmother's body, ran out of the room and down the hallway. I'll never forget the sight of that horrid cat, squatting there on my dead grandmother. It gave me the willies. It's something that I've seen in my dreams for years. And ever since then, I've hated cats. I won't even go near them."

Felidae certainly have had their share of bad press. Cats are blamed for a variety of evils, especially in the days when superstition—like the shadows of twilight—brought out man's worst fears. The folklore of Knoxville, and all of East Tennessee for that matter, is rife with legends of cats—both good and evil.

In an earlier book of mine (*Demon in the Woods*), I told of bizarre sightings of a strange animal—a catlike creature that walked on two legs. A person told me of hearing a strange scratching noise late one night coming from the little vegetable garden growing in his backyard in Knoxville. He thought the sound came from neighborhood dogs digging up his pole beans. He had had trouble with dogs before, but the local police would never do anything about the problem.

After hearing the noise, he got out of bed and walked to the back door, prepared to chase the offending canines with some well-aimed rocks. Instead he saw two gleaming catlike eyes rise from behind his vegetables. Then he heard a hiss like an angry cat at bay. Thoroughly spooked—perhaps thinking that a mountain lion had somehow escaped from the Knoxville Zoo and was lurking in his garden—the man turned on his heel and scurried back inside the house. He said that he never saw the strange beast again—nor did he ever want to.

What our friend might have seen was a Wampas Cat—an enigmatic beast said to roam East Tennessee and Southwest Virginia. Sightings occur mainly at night or twilight. Sometimes seen are a pair of glowing yellow eyes; sometimes, a glimpse of a fleeing shadow. And sometimes there is nothing more than a low, menacing growl. But on occasion the cat is clearly seen—perhaps too clearly!

Since my original stories were published, I have heard from a number of other people who also claim to have seen the Wampas Cat. One of my informants was a student at the University of Tennessee who said she saw the creature one night perched on "The Hill":

"The moon was out and it was kind of chilly," she wrote me recently. "I was walking along and I saw this animal sitting there in the middle of the grass, looking across the river. At first I thought it was a dog—it was big enough. I love dogs so, naturally, I called to it. When it turned I saw that it was no dog. It was a big cat—bigger than any I have ever seen before. It screamed at the top of its voice, jumped up, and—I swear—ran off on two legs!"

I think that the legend of the Wampas Cat has its origin in ancient Cherokee folklore. As the tale was told to me several years ago in North Carolina, a demon was lurking near the Cherokee town of Etowah (or Chota, depending on the version you hear). All night long it screamed, keeping the entire village awake and shaking in its collective moccasins. Finally, when it was decided that the demon apparently had no intentions of leaving, one of the bravest of the braves ventured out into the woods to chase it off. The catch was this: he had to spot the demon before it spotted him. If the horrible creature saw him first, the sight of it would drive him crazy. Unfortunately the demon saw him before he saw it and scared the Indian so much that the brave was instantly transformed into a drooling lunatic.

The hapless brave's wife, a diminutive woman with apparently more spunk than brains, claimed the right to confront the demon and avenge her husband. Before she ventured out into the woods, however, a kindly medicine man gave her the face of a wildcat that had been tanned into a so-called "booger mask," worn to frighten bad spirits away from town meetings in the council house.

Unlike her husband, the woman was successful in sneaking up on the unholy beast. She screamed bloody murder to get the demon's attention. The startled demon turned, and the sight of the booger mask terrified it so much that the hideous monster let out a roar and fled into the woods, never to be seen again in the vicinity.

Ever since that time, or so the legend goes, the ghost of the Cherokee woman, still wearing the booger mask, roams East Tennessee, Western North Carolina, and Southwest Virginia, looking for demons to expatriate. And I think, from this nearly forgotten Cherokee tale springs the modern legend of the Wampas Cat.

Being principally of Celtic heritage, early East Tennesseans were, as a people, generally superstitious and therefore noticeably uneasy around cats. Few felines were kept as pets. The Reverend Samuel Doak, the first Presbyterian clergyman to venture into East Tennessee, wrote in a letter that the "pious must resist such an evil creature." Doak's counsel was not too surprising considering the history of the beast.

The so-called "tiger on the hearth" has a long and checkered history. At various times the cat has been considered either a holy or diabolical beast, a bringer of good fortune, or a curse on humanity.

In ancient Egypt and Babylonia, for example, cats were

considered sacred. One Egyptian god in particular, Pasht, was not only cat-headed, but was attended by cats. To kill a cat in Egypt was to commit high sacrilege and could very well cause the culprit to be put to the sword. In fact, in the land of the Pharaohs, a black cat crossing one's path was considered to be good luck! Archaeologists have even unearthed mummies of cats from royal tombs in the Valley of the Kings, buried right beside members of the royal family.

Events did not go well for cats when the Middle Ages rolled around. In the religious frenzy of the time, cats—especially black cats—were considered mystical and familiar spirits of the devil. Witches were said to be accompanied by cats in their mischief-making. Sometimes the witches even took the shape of cats so that they could slink around unnoticed.

Norse mythology includes the story of a witch, Freya, who had a chariot pulled by black cats that turned, when they took the notion, into black horses. These changelings were very fast because they were said, like their mistress, to be possessed of the devil. Witches' cats also were said, at times, to have the power of speech and to be able to predict the future.

In the Middle Ages, felines were sometimes hunted down and killed like murderers on the lam. And if its owner was convicted of witchcraft and condemned to die, there was a good chance that he or she would be accompanied to the gallows by the cat which would also be hung right beside him/her.

Although few cats are lynched today as minions of the devil, they still retain that certain unsettling mystique that causes uneasiness around them. Perhaps it is their independent nature that prompts the belief that cats have supernormal powers, or maybe it's their intense, unblinking stare that spooks people. Who knows? At any rate, cats are the subject of numerous widespread superstitions that have sprung up around them over the years. Here are a few examples which are not, I may add, exclusive to East Tennessee:

• If a black cat crosses your path, evil will soon befall you.
• If a cat leaves home while a person is sick and cannot

be coaxed back, the person will die.

• Tortoiseshell cats are considered lucky in Great Britain.

• If cats run around wildly, expect a wind to blow up.

• If a cat sneezes near the bride-to-be on the morning of the wedding, she will have a happy life.

• Stroking the tail of a black cat will cure a sty in the eye.

• Cats found lurking in coal mines are considered to be bad luck.

• A dried cat skin is a good cure for a toothache. (YUK!)

John Sevier, Tennessee's legendary Indian fighter and the state's first governor, was reportedly fond of cats. Being of French Huguenot descent, he possessed many of the same built-in prejudices that afflicted his Scottish and Irish brethren. Both groups followed Calvinist doctrine. But Sevier was always his own man, not one to succumb to the herd mentality. In a letter to his friend Isaac Shelby, Sevier mentions "the wonderful comfort" the sight of his tabby stretched out on the warm hearth offered. Maybe Sevier was the first cat lover in East Tennessee.

Another Knoxville-area cat, which afforded a lot less comfort and once caused an area-wide epidemic of the heebie-jeebies, belonged to a midwife who lived in a little run-down shack about six miles from town. In the days just before the War Between the States, midwives were considered a little like the lawyers of today—they were to be avoided unless you were in desperate need of their services; then you engaged them very grudgingly. This was because many midwives were considered witches. Some even brewed potions for all sorts of magical purposes and were said to be in league with the devil.

One particular midwife—the Widow Jennings was her name—lived alone in a little cabin in a thick grove of trees. Only the very desperate—or the very foolhardy—would beat a path to her door. In cases when a doctor was not available to deliver a child, however, it was the Widow Jennings who was summoned to the bedside. During the occupation of Knoxville by Confederate troops, Unionists even claimed that local physician Dr. Henry Baker, himself (see "Ghosts of the

Baker-Peters House" later in this book), would consult with the Widow Jennings on a host of sticky medical problems.

It would also seem that the Widow Jennings was considered a bit of a heart specialist. If a young lady was having difficulty in obtaining a husband, she would go see the good Widow for a potion that would attract the proper man into her life.

The problem was that the Widow Jennings was a lonely woman who enjoyed the notoriety she attracted. She simply couldn't keep her big mouth shut. She would even brag about midnight cavorts with Satan himself. She claimed that she met him in the woods near her house and he would reveal black magic rites to keep her own magic powerful.

This vaunting didn't sit well with some of the rock-solid religious types in the community, and they decided that Knox County would be well rid of this alleged minion of the devil. One night they gathered their forces and marched out of town—torches blazing—by horse, wagon, and foot, like a righteous army of God. Six miles later the mob reached the little grove of trees where the Widow Jennings had her cabin.

Even with the force of overwhelming numbers, however, they were still afraid of the devil's power they thought the Widow possessed. They decided, therefore, that it was prudent not to storm the door. No telling what kind of evil was in the cabin with the old witch. Maybe even the "prince of flies" himself was present. So they loitered outside her door, taunting the Widow to come out and get what was coming to her. But all was quiet inside the cabin. Nothing stirred. Not a sound.

"Come out of there, Widow Jennings," one of the men shouted. "We want to reckon with you."

Still no answer.

Then the mob heard a strange noise from the side of the cabin—like the hiss of an angry cat. They saw a pair of enormous yellow eyes reflected in the light of their torches. Then a huge red mouth, filled with sharp teeth, snarled at them in the darkness.

It was her cat—at least it looked like the Widow Jennings's

cat. But this one was huge. It must have stood six feet at the shoulder. And it had the look of pure evil about it. It was crouching, every muscle in its body taut and ready to spring.

Some of the saddle horses reared in terror, turned, and bolted down the road, closely followed by other animals pulling wagons and carriages, then the mob. They didn't stop until they reached the safety of their homes and barns.

And the Widow Jennings was never bothered again.

Some say the monster which confronted the mob in the front yard of the Widow Jennings's house that terrifying night was a panther ("painter," as they called it) who had blundered onto the scene and, in the darkness, was perceived to be larger than it really was. But those clucking tongues who had urged the mob in the first place were certain that they knew the truth of the matter. The creature was the Widow's own cat, made huge by black magic—black magic learned at the feet of the devil and conjured up by the devil's own hand-maiden, herself!

"Is That You, Abner?"
The Ghost(s) of the Baker-Peters House

Maybe there are two ghosts haunting the old Baker-Peters house in West Knoxville. Maybe there is just one. Any way you cut it, however, there are some pretty weird goings-on in that house. Most folks favor the shade of young Abner Baker. But his father, Dr. Harvey Baker, may also be involved. It goes without saying, however, that both are prime candidates to be ghosts. Both died violent deaths.

Folks who study the paranormal on a "scientific" basis say that a person who has a very strong personality, or dies before his time, or dies in an unhappy state of mind (like in mourning for a lost love) has the best chance of becoming a haunt after he departs the present dimension. In the South, apparently, this is especially true because of the bucolic nature of the area. Hans Holzer, in his book *The Phantoms of Dixie*, explains:

"The slower, more tradition-bound atmosphere of the Southern states tends to encourage a preoccupation with the occult," he writes. "The Southern states are less polyglot and in the main populated by people of Anglo-Saxon extraction. Now it is a fact that the Scottish, English, and Irish people have a greater leaning toward the psychic than have, let us say, the French or German nationals. Why this is so is difficult to determine unless, indeed, the Celtic heritage still pulsates in so many of these people. From their ancestral homes in the British Isles many of these Southerners have derived a respect for the occult which makes them more receptive to reports dealing with occurrences of seemingly logical events. The atmosphere for ghosts, hauntings, psychic dreams and such is far more open in the South than in the urban North."

Okay. We'll accept that explanation for the time being, mainly because it agrees with what we've been saying all along about our East Tennessee heritage. It really is bucolic and tradition-bound. So how does this theory apply to the unearthly Bakers of Knoxville? Why, in the classic sense, did they become ghosts? And even more important, why did they die such horrible deaths?

Physician Harvey Baker moved to Knoxville in 1840 and built his two-story, red brick house on Kingston Pike at Baker's Creek, then no more than a muddy wagon track snaking out of town. There he prospered and grew wealthy. He was a convenient godsend to those far removed from the town. He cured the sick, delivered babies, and attended the dying. He was respected not only for his skill as a doctor, but for his humanity—but not for his politics.

As the War Between the States approached, the people of Knox County were, for the most part, staunchly pro-Union. Even those who possessed slaves—and they were few in East Tennessee—saw the advantage of preserving the Union and opposing secession. When Tennessee voted to leave the Union on June 8, 1861, most of the pro votes came from Middle and West Tennessee, where a slave-based workforce on the flatlands was more practical than in the rugged East Tennessee mountains. There was even a movement begun for the counties of East Tennessee to secede from the rest of the state and form their own political boundaries and join the Union themselves, and they noted with more than casual interest what their uneasy neighbors to the north were about to do.

The western Virginians caused no end of embarrassment for the eastern, and Confederate, portions of the state. These anti-Confederate rebels in 1861—traitors to the cause, if you will—were holding Congressional seats once held by eastern Virginians. Furthermore, the territory that they wanted to make a loyal Union state was bordered by the Ohio River, a strategic waterway that skirted Kentucky and emptied into the Mississippi River. The loss of Kentucky would do irreparable damage to the Confederacy.

Jefferson Davis dispatched Robert E. Lee to the west to try to preserve western Virginia for the Confederacy. Lee, who was to act only as an advisor to the four small armies already in the field, was met with hostility—not only by residents, but by his own commanders. A three-month campaign yielded not a single battle; in each instance the enemy vacated the field unobserved, leaving the Confederates staring at a mountainous landscape containing nothing more than an occasional irate farmer armed with a pitchfork.

The result of this bloodless campaign was that Lee (this, of course, was before he achieved phenomenal success as the commander of the Army of Northern Virginia) was perceived by the Southern press as being too cautious or tender-hearted to send his troops into battle. Thus he was dubbed "Granny Lee" or "Evacuating Lee."

As the secession vote approached in Tennessee, *Brownlow's Knoxville Whig* called for pro-Union delegates to gather in the city on May 30. The resulting three-day convention, held out in the open near Temperance Hall, drew unionists from all over the state. Fiery speeches rained down like sulfur and brimstone—resist secession, preserve the Union! East Tennessee was in a similar situation as western Virginia. Not only was there the Tennessee River to consider, but the mountains were strategic because they yielded grain and cattle, unlike the one-crop farming of cotton farther to the south.

Brownlow's Knoxville Whig's main reason for existence was its editorial page. The paper's zealous editor, William Gannaway "Parson" Brownlow, wrote explosive editorials. He never minced words, and the only view that counted was Brownlow's (which, in his opinion, was infallible). His readers loved the Parson's pungent prose, and the *Whig* found distribution far beyond the city limits of Knoxville.

Brownlow was unalterably pro-Union, and after South Carolina seceded from the union, and even before Tennessee did likewise (it was, in fact, the last Southern state to do so), new *Whig* subscriptions had already started coming in from

PREACHER WITH AN ATTITUDE

William Gannaway "Parson" Brownlow—clergyman, fiery orator, unalterable abolitionist, explosive editorialist, and future Tennessee governor—defied the Confederate occupation of Knoxville by flying the Union Stars and Stripes over his house in full view of Rebel soldiers. His subsequent arrest caused great embarrassment for Jefferson Davis and the Confederate government.

the North. Brownlow's already massive ego reveled in this notoriety, and his pen became even more vitriolic. The Parson and his traitorous rag were prickly thorns in the side of the Confederacy.

In 1861 Knoxville was occupied by Confederate forces, and the situation began to get a bit uncomfortable for the defiant Parson, especially since he insisted in continuing to fly the Stars and Stripes over his house instead of the Stars and Bars. The situation was further aggravated when, two days after the election of Jefferson Davis and Alexander Stephens as president and vice-president of the Confederacy, a number of bridges were torched in the East Tennessee mountains. Armed citizens prepared to march to Cumberland Gap, where they expected to meet and join up with Union troops coming out of Kentucky. A much annoyed Davis sent troops to squash the rebellion, ordering the arrest and lynching of anyone found guilty of burning bridges. Five men were eventually hanged, while others were held without benefit of a trial.

Among those jailed was Parson Brownlow, although it was never proved that he took an active part in the burnings. However, the incarceration of Brownlow, who was by now nationally known, proved another embarrassment for Davis; and to save face, he was forced to release the prisoner. Brownlow was escorted through the Union lines and out of the Confederacy. Davis hoped the deportation was permanent.

The occupation of Knoxville by rebels, conversely, made life a little easier for Dr. Baker. His son, Abner, had already marched off to join the Confederate army, and the occupational forces knew of Dr. Baker's loyalties and treated him accordingly. The doctor had even turned his home on Kingston Pike into a makeshift hospital to treat wounded soldiers. Unfortunately for Dr. Baker, Confederate forces were unable to hold the town, and when the tide of occupation shifted in 1863, so did the doctor's fortunes.

Knoxville was now a Union stronghold. General Ambrose E. Burnside was the commander. It didn't take long for Burnside to realize which side Dr. Baker was on. The doctor continued to treat wounded Confederate soldiers during the first day of Union occupation. But when the plot was finally discovered, Burnside gave orders for Dr. Baker's immediate arrest.

One morning Dr. Baker looked out his front window and saw a large body of belligerent Union soldiers approaching. Leaving his wife to tend to the few Confederate soldiers still in his care (no one would dare harm a helpless woman, he probably thought), Dr. Baker burst out of the back door and jumped on his horse. The soldiers opened fire with their Springfields. Lead buzzed hot and heavy. The horse was hit and went down with a grunt in a cloud of dust. Dr. Baker leaped to his feet, turned, and ran back into the house, barricading himself in a second-floor bedroom.

Union soldiers stormed the front porch and broke in the front door. Then they stampeded up the stairs, demanding that the doctor surrender. Baker refused. Several of the sol-

THE UNION GENERAL WHO LEFT A "HAIRLOOM"

Major General Ambrose E. Burnside commanded Union troops during the occupation of Knoxville. Usually an affable, even-tempered individual, Burnside's patience was sorely tested when it was discovered that a local physician was giving aid and comfort to the enemy. *Note: The general's distinctive mutton chops were dubbed by his troops as "Burnsides" and, later, "sideburns." This facial brush, of course, became quite fashionable during the War Between the States; and in a slightly abbreviated form, their popularity continued far into the twentieth century.*

diers fired through the bolted bedroom door. One of the minié balls tore through the wood and buried itself in Dr. Baker's chest, killing him.

The saga of Dr. Harvey Baker was over. His bloody body was dragged away and buried. His distraught wife eventually remarried. End of story, right?

Wrong!

As I said at the beginning of this chapter, there might be two ghosts haunting the Baker-Peters House. Dr. Baker's son, Abner, went off to fight with the Confederates and returned to Knoxville in 1865, and he was an "unreconstructed" rebel. Vengeance was on his mind, and he was determined to inflict his own brand of justice on those "dirty Yankees" who had killed his father.

There are a number of versions of how Abner died; neither one is very pleasant. In her book, *Knoxville*, Betsey Beeler Creekmore says that after the war came to an end, Abner, a man small in stature, continued to hold Confederate sympathies. As was the fashion of the times in Knoxville, Abner always went armed.

One day he got into an argument with William Hall, clerk of the Knox County Court, a big man who always carried a cane. Words soon turned to blows. As a crowd gathered to watch the fracas, the clerk whacked Abner across the face with his cane. His face stinging from the blow, Abner drew his pistol and shot the clerk dead before the horrified crowd.

Suddenly the crowd became a mob. They knew Abner's unpopular Confederate sympathies, and they remembered that his father had died as a traitor trying to escape his Union captors. Besides that, the clerk that Abner had suddenly dispatched was a popular man in town. So the howling mob collared Abner and dragged him up to Hill Street to a tree on the edge of property owned by Colonel Perez Dickinson. They threw a rope over a convenient branch, then asked Abner if he had any last words.

"Yes!" the ever defiant Abner said. "Now watch a rebel die."

And they did.

And now, another version: *Knoxville News-Sentinel* columnist Sam Venable wrote in 1986 that Hall was not inside the courthouse when Abner arrived. Instead he was bending an elbow in the Mansion House saloon. He glanced out the window and saw Abner walk into the courthouse. Hall knew that Abner thought that Hall had ridden with the troops that had killed his father and that the son had sworn vengeance on the culprits. Now the time had come for a showdown. Before leaving the saloon and going after Abner inside the courthouse, Hall boasted to his friends that they were about to witness "the damnedest thrashing ever a white man ever got."

According to Venable, Hall "flew into the little man with his cane, striking him over the head and arms. Then with fists flying they tumbled down the stairs and into the street. As Hall raised his hand for another blow, Baker drew a pistol. He fired one shot. It struck Hall in the head, killing him instantly."

A third version of the death of Abner Baker is told by Ian

Winton, writing in the *Knoxville Journal*, retelling a story that he had gotten from architect Gene Burr of the Knoxville Heritage Association. According to this version it was not the clerk of the county court who inspired Abner's wrath. Apparently Abner was well aware of the identity of the participants in the raid that killed his father. One of these was none other than the postmaster of Knoxville.

In September 1865, Abner walked down to the post office with blood in his eyes and killed the postmaster. When he tried to escape he was caught by the postmaster's friends, tied behind a team of horses, and dragged around the streets of Knoxville until he was dead.

Whatever story you choose to believe is not important here. Abner killed and, in turn, was killed. The fact is that his memory was little tarnished by his crime. The East Tennessee Daughters of the American Revolution placed a plaque outside the Baker-Peters house in 1926, proclaiming Abner a "martyr for manliness."

And so Abner or his father—or both—haunt the Baker-Peters House on Kingston Pike. The bullet-ridden door, behind which Dr. Baker died, still hangs on its jamb. The house has played host to a number of restaurants over the years, and nearly all owners have experienced ghostly happenings. Yvonne Loveday, a former correspondent for the *News-Sentinel* who is now with University Relations at the University of Tennessee, tells the story of one of these owners who mistook ghostly activity for a burglary and about the mystified police officers who tried to solve the crime.

Writing in the *News-Sentinel*, she said that the manager of Abner's Attic Restaurant, Rex Jones, called the police when it was discovered that a tape cassette player, some fine wine, and cash were missing. Furthermore, a heavy glass ashtray had been chucked through a half-inch-thick glass window on the second floor.

When detectives dusted for prints, they found nothing, not even a smudge. Impossible. There had to be something. After all, any intruder would have had to climb a set of stairs and stand on a roof in order to gain entry. Finally the detectives gave up and, in their report, listed the suspect as "unknown." Case unsolved.

Ironically, it was manager Jones who solved his own mystery. He later found all the missing items—not actually stolen but "rearranged." The stereo had been moved to another shelf; the wine bottles had been moved from one table to another. And the money had also been moved to a different location. No one would admit to having moved the items, and the only thing that Jones could figure was that the ghost of Abner, or his father, had been the culprit. Even in death they seem to have retained their sense of humor.

And that's what goes on at the Baker-Peters House—the ghosts are mischievous, not malicious. The haunting consists of poltergeist activity. No visible specters are ever seen. Restaurant owners have reported mysterious voices, screams, and mumbling coming from the attic. Boxes and jars fly off shelves and land several feet away from their take-off point. Other kinds of noises plague the old building—creaks, snaps, crackles, and the sounds of footfalls. Lights flick on and off. Electrical appliances are turned on and off by unseen hands.

One of the strangest events of all was the time that Jones arrived one morning and found one arm of a solid brass chandelier bent out of shape. It actually had to be reheated to be fixed.

One person told me that strange yellow lights appear in the windows of the Baker-Peters House at night when no one is there. He said that the lights look exactly like kerosene lanterns being carried from room to room. Maybe they are being carried by the ghost of Dr. Baker, still caring for the sick but now far out of reach of real human suffering.

Or maybe Hans Holzer would have a better explanation.

Underground Knoxville

The theme of time travel has intrigued people for years, especially when they get a chance to journey back to a nostalgic, less complicated time. I remember one such story concerning Grand Central Station in New York City. Some of the railway tunnels beneath the building were unused and forgotten for years. Two men decided to investigate one of the lower tunnels one day, and while they were exploring, they heard a train whistle. Before long, an ancient steam engine chugged around the bend.

One of the men decided to conduct a dangerous experiment. As the ghost train from the past roared by, he jumped into the apparition. When the train had passed, the man was nowhere to be seen.

Later that day his puzzled companion returned home and, by chance, found an old letter in his grandfather's trunk that contained family heirlooms. It was signed by the man who had jumped into the ghost train. Apparently he had traveled back in time to turn-of-the-century Ohio, where he had started a little feed and grain business. He reported that he was very happy and very content. He had written the letter and stashed it in a place where he knew his friend would one day find it—in an old trunk belonging to his grandfather!

Gay Street seems to have the same kind of effect on some people—a tangible symbol of a bygone time. One day, not too many years ago, a man was walking down Gay Street when he happened to come upon a mule and cart standing by the curb. Considering that it was the middle of the 1980s, the man thought the sight a bit strange. After all, mules were a rare sight on the Knox County landscape, especially in the city. So what was the animal doing there in the middle of traffic?

The man got his answer in a rather unexpected way. A car pulled up to the curb to park, running right through the cart and animal, which then disappeared into thin air.

The man asked the driver of the car if he had seen a mule. "Are you crazy, Mister?" the driver said. "There aren't any mules in Knoxville these days." Then he walked away shaking his head.

But the fellow on the curb was sure that he had seen the mule and the cart, and that his eyes were not playing tricks on him.

This is but one of the strange incidents that seem to center around Gay Street, the main business artery in downtown Knoxville. Gay Street, named for a thoroughfare in Philadelphia, was one of the original ten streets laid out by Charles McClung in the 1791 plan of the new capital of the Southwest Territory.

Once upon a time, Gay Street was a lot more hilly than it is today. In fact it went up and down like a rumpled sheet and was not, at all, the kind of broad, smooth main street that Knoxvillians could point to with pride. So, sometime in the late nineteenth century, thousands of tons of fill were brought in to make "the rough places plain." This led to a widespread belief that the fill dirt was poured in rather quickly and that another Knoxville—complete with turn of the century storefronts, lampposts, and other relics of the past—is sequestered beneath present street level, just like the cities of Pompeii and Herculaneum when Mt. Vesuvius buried them in AD 79, or like the old railroad tunnels beneath Grand Central Station.

Of course the city denies anything like this is possible, but there have been some mighty odd things happen along that thoroughfare. One day in the early twentieth century, some of the locals were lounging outside Schubert's Saloon when they saw Gay Street begin to undulate. The movement was described as a giant mole burrowing its way up the street. The spectacle was enough to make a man swear off strong drink for life. When the excitement subsided, however, it was

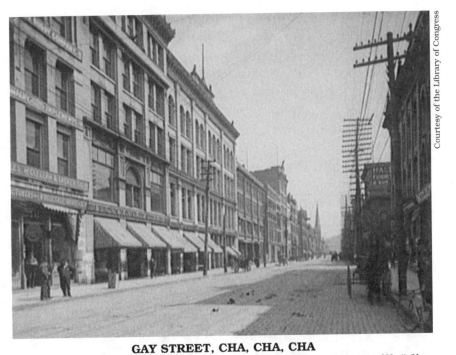

GAY STREET, CHA, CHA, CHA
Not only are there persistent rumors that a buried "Knoxville" lies beneath Gay Street, but about the time this photograph was taken, the entire street began to rock and roll as if a giant worm was tunneling beneath the brick paving. The spectacle nearly forced patrons of nearby Schubert's Saloon to give up strong drink forever.

discovered that the mysterious movement was due to an underground water main that had broken.

Speaking of the action of water, it is a well-known fact that the limestone beneath the streets of Knoxville is honeycombed with caves. Their network is so extensive that one is said to even burrow all the way beneath the Tennessee River, though the existence of such a cave is highly unlikely. The truth is, however, that the caves of Knoxville were once used as part of the Underground Railroad. Now some of the passages are said to be haunted by the ghosts of former slaves.

Perez Dickinson, whose money and influence helped shape the fortunes of Knoxville during Reconstruction, was not always held in such high esteem by his townsmen. He had come to Knoxville from Massachusetts in 1830, the ink on his Amherst College diploma barely dry. No sooner had

Dickinson arrived in Knoxville than the trustees of Hampden-Sydney Academy recruited him to teach their students and to serve as principal—a heady assignment for a boy of only seventeen. However, Perez longed for greener pastures, and a few years after his arrival he resigned his post at the school and went into the retail business with James H. Cowan, his brother-in-law. It was inevitable their flourishing concern would expand, and shortly thereafter the partners joined with Charles and Frank McClung in the wholesale business.

In keeping with his newfound prosperity, Perez built a fine house on Main Street. Then he took a bride. Unfortunately she and an infant son died the day after the child was born.

As Perez grew richer, he grew bolder. Influenced by the writings of New Englander William Lloyd Garrison, he became a staunch abolitionist. Then he got the notion that an anti-slavery newspaper should be published in the South. That way, anti-slave propaganda would reach more slave-holders and might serve to influence them. At the same time, Perez found himself at odds with both the editorial policy and the literary content of the incumbent Knoxville newspaper. So he and a few like-minded young men proceeded to publish their own paper—the twice weekly *Knoxville Times*.

Unlike "Parson" Brownlow, however, Perez was no rabble-rouser. In fact his editor, Thomas Humes, put more emphasis on the literary content of the paper than on flaming editorials.

As the threat of Southern secession became an inevitability, Perez turned his thoughts into action. The first thing that he did was build a tunnel. The second thing that he did was enlist his family as decoys.

Perez wasn't so much pro-Union as he was anti-slavery. Unlike Brownlow, however, Perez mostly kept his opinions to himself. Confederate elements in Knoxville were, of course, dimly aware of his abolitionist tendencies but considered him harmless. All that he owned and had worked for, as considerable as it might be, was in Knoxville. Why would a successful businessman risk all of that for an unpopular idea?

Yes, indeed. They were convinced that Perez Dickinson was content to mind the store as well as tend to his knitting.

What they didn't know was that their tight-lipped neighbor busied himself by burrowing like a mole through the limestone beneath his house, trying to connect with the natural limestone caves that ran down to the Tennessee River. As far as the knitting was concerned, he had convinced some of the members of his large family to do just that as a diversion to his subterranean activities.

Perez Dickinson's fine house was built on extensive cellars that would make the Paris Opera House green with envy. And the white porticoed structure was only two blocks from the Tennessee River. It was a simple matter to connect his cellar with one of the natural limestone caves so that he could smuggle runaway slaves to freedom. In the meantime, Perez's nieces would sit on the porch with their knitting or needlepoint, giving the unmistakable impression of domestic tranquility while masking the clandestine activity beneath their feet.

There is some question—not to mention mystery—as to the exact escape route used. Legend has it that there was a cave that went all the way under the Tennessee River—from the Cherokee Bluffs to Chilhowee Park. Slaves would be led through the dark passage all the way across the river to safety. Geologists, however, will claim that this is an impossibility. A more feasible route would have been underground to the bank of the river, then by boat or raft to the other side.

When Southern troops came to occupy Knoxville—and especially in the days just after the infamous bridge burnings in East Tennessee by Union sympathizers—Perez thought it best to remove himself and his family from the town. They traveled north to Jonesborough and waited until it was safe.

The family returned in the early part of 1863 when Union troops, under the command of Major General Ambrose E. Burnside, held the town. Perez's house was a shambles, having been occupied at one time or the other by both Confederate and Union troops. But, surprisingly, no one had found his tunnel. Later, during Reconstruction, he would use that tunnel to hide blacks from the rampaging Ku Klux Klan.

Perez Dickinson died in 1901. Today, according to Betsey Beeler Creekmore, "nothing is left of Perez Dickinson except his influence on the city in his time." The house is gone and the tunnel is forgotten. But the legend lives on.

Many an adventurous (and, we add, foolhardy) lad has found his way into those caverns used by Perez Dickinson to smuggle slaves to freedom. The young adventurers return with strange stories of voices—ancient voices—coming from the darkness. One of the best known of these tales concerns a young man who, with two cronies, decided one day in the 1920s to explore Knoxville's underground. Without entertaining a moment's thought that they might be putting their lives in terrible danger by exploring an undeveloped cave, the group slithered through an opening on a hillside and found themselves standing in a narrow passageway.

As they made their way through the dank passage, their only light came from the few candles they had brought with them. Above their heads they could barely see stalactites hanging from the ceiling. The floor was strewn with rocks, and they had to step carefully lest they trip and fall.

Several minutes passed. The passage became narrower, now barely wide enough for the boys to pass through sideways. Still they continued, not even considering the possibility of suddenly plunging into a gaping pit and being killed for their recklessness. Luckily for them, the rock remained firm under their feet.

Finally the boys emerged into what appeared to be a large room. Now they couldn't see the ceiling at all in the dim glow of their candles, nor could they see the far wall. Then a sudden, mysterious breeze blew out their candles.

It was pitch black—total darkness. There was no sound except for the steady drip-drip of water. As the boys fumbled for their matches, they heard muffled voices. Then a faint glow appeared in a side corridor. The voices grew louder.

"Who is down here with us?" the boys asked as they glanced at each other nervously.

Then a man appeared, holding a torch. He wore dark, old-fashioned clothes. Behind him came a black man, then a black woman, and another black man—all in single file. The boys hunkered down behind a rock and anxiously watched the strange procession. There were a dozen or so blacks following the white man with the torch. All were dressed in seedy clothing. The boys thought that they looked just like... SLAVES!!!!

It was then that the two lads fully understood what they were witnessing. These were ghosts from the past, slaves being led to freedom by none other than the spirit of Perez Dickinson himself!

Try as we might, some of us never get over our fear of horrible creatures under the bed. There, lurking among the dust balls, are all manner of monstrosities that prefer to do their dirty work when the lights go out. The time-honored bogeyman is such a creature. So is the slimy soul sucker. Childhood fear of monsters waiting to prey on the unsuspecting is supposed to disappear with maturity. Yet some never get over their fear of the dark, nor of the denizens that supposedly roam the shadows.

In 1994 Jack Neely wrote in *Metro Pulse* about the so-called "Beast of Middlebrook." Those who have seen the creature say that it is snow white and about twice the size of a large dog. Some claim that it is actually an albino black bear. Apparently the creature has been around many years, but the legend took on a new twist in the summer of 1994. Apparently the heads of dead cattle began disappearing from Middlebrook slaughtering pens. A very unusual string of thefts, to say the least. Some thought the culprits were members of some sort of devil cult who used the heads in an unholy ceremony. Others thought that a panther was on the prowl in west Knoxville. Still more blamed the missing heads on the "Beast of Middlebrook."

Another Knoxville area beast is "Lonesome Jack." Jack, as some folks tell it, was a whiskey drummer who was waylayed sometime during the War Between the States and robbed of his samples and his money. Then he was murdered.

The ghost of Jack wanders the woods at night, just outside Knoxville, looking for his property. He occasionally will approach a house, knock on a window, and peer inside. Since Jack was killed by a blow to the head with the butt of an Enfield rifle, his ghost comes complete with a gaping head wound. He is not a pretty sight and certainly not something that a person would want to see gawking in his window on a dark and stormy night.

Is it possible that there is a monster—or possibly two—who lurks beneath the streets of Knoxville? As mentioned in a previous chapter, it is well known that the limestone beneath downtown Knoxville is honeycombed with caves—miles and miles of dark, dank passages, most of which have been unmapped and uncharted. Although Perez Dickinson used one of these passages to transport runaway slaves from his home to the Tennessee River, it is doubtful that he was familiar with more than one or two of the caverns. Although he reported no unusual creatures lurking there, there still comes the story of a monster that lives underground and who, occasionally, ventures into the outer world.

Since bears use caves as dens, the creature is naturally assumed to be a bear. But this is not just any bear. By all reports, it is over fifteen feet tall! No bear is that big—not even a grizzly and certainly not a black bear. That fact, however, does not quell the legend, and sometimes a great hairy monster is reported walking Gay Street in the dark of the night. At other times, oddly enough, the mysterious figure is not described as a bear at all—but rather the form of an ancient Indian.

How did such a story get started? A journalist friend of mine in Knoxville told me the following tale:

Back in the days when James White was building his fort, and the land surrounding Knoxville was nothing but wilderness, a long hunter was stalking a deer through the woods. Suddenly he came upon a bear. Winter was coming on and the hunter needed a robe to keep him warm, so he forgot all about the deer that he was hunting and took off after the bear. The animal would provide both a warm robe and meat.

The terrified animal lumbered through the thick forest, just a few steps ahead of the hunter. Finally it got to the banks of the Tennessee River and started running at the water's edge. The hunter kept up his pursuit but was slowing down because he was beginning to tire. Finally he could go no farther and sat down on a large rock to rest. The bear, of course, was getting away, but the hunter knew that he would have no trouble picking up his trail. It was only a matter of time until he caught up with the animal again.

Sure enough, when the hunter resumed the chase, the bear's tracks were clearly stamped in the river mud. A short distance later the tracks turned away from the river and headed toward a bluff. A few yards after that the hunter came upon the mouth of a large cave. The tracks disappeared into the opening. The hunter stopped and peered into the darkness. He could see only about fifty feet past the entrance, but the bear was nowhere in sight. Suddenly he was amazed to see an ancient Indian medicine man step out behind a rock. He was very short, very thin, and was wearing only a loincloth. His eyes were extraordinarily pale and his long white hair hung down well below his waist. In his hand he held a hickory staff. He stopped just short of the long hunter and tapped the end of the staff on the ground three times.

"White man," he said in a gnarled voice. "Are you looking for brother bear?"

The startled long hunter could only stammer out a "yes."

"He is there," the old Indian said, pointing with his staff. "In the cave. He awaits you."

The long hunter stared into the darkness, but he couldn't see anything but blackness. He eyed the old Indian suspiciously. "You saw him go past?" the long hunter asked.

"He is in the cave," the Indian repeated.

Suddenly the air was shattered by a mighty roar. By the sound of it, the bear was quite a bit larger than the one that the long hunter remembered. Instantly the appeal of bear meat left him. Moreover, the robe that he envisioned himself wearing during the coming winter did not seem quite so warm. The long hunter began backing up. It was one thing to fight a bear in the woods in the daylight and quite another to do battle inside a dark cave where he couldn't see his hand in front of his face.

"Brother bear is waiting," said the old medicine man. "Are you not going to fight him. Are you not a noble warrior? Are you a coward that shoots in the back? This cave is his home and he will defend it and himself as well. Will you fight him on his ground?"

"Not today," the long hunter said as he turned to walk away.

The old Indian said nothing, but smiled slightly. He stood stone still at the mouth of the cave, the hickory staff in his hand. Another roar was heard from inside the cave—this one not as fierce as the last. The hunter turned again. He saw nothing but darkness inside. The old Indian continued to stand at the mouth, staring into the white man's eyes with a smiling expression that gave the long hunter the creeps. Then the white man continued his retreat from the cave. He couldn't get the medicine man out of his mind. Where had he come from so suddenly? He burned with curiosity.

The long hunter walked about 150 yards, then he suddenly ducked behind a thick bush. He peered from behind the foliage at the cave entrance. The old Indian continued to stand at the mouth, the staff still in his hands. Then the air around the old man began to shimmer and the figure began to grow in size and bulk. Slowly it lost its human shape. The staff fell to the ground with a clatter. The old man had magically turned into an enormous black bear.

The bear stood on its haunches and gave a mighty roar. Presently the smaller bear—the one that the now thoroughly frightened long hunter had been pursuing—appeared at the opening. It looked up at the huge bear in awe. The big bear roared again, and the smaller animal tentatively ventured into the woods.

Now would be a good time for the long hunter—once he got over his fright—to continue his hunt. Perhaps he could waylay the animal and kill it before it could run. And he might have followed such a plan except for one small detail. As the small bear disappeared into the brush, the large bear looked directly at the spot where the long hunter was hiding, opened its mouth, and in a half hiss/half roar plainly growled, "BROOOTHER BEARRRRR!"

The beast knew full well that the white man was watching, and delivered a final warning!

The Cherokee Indians, of course, believed that everything in nature had a spirit—the wind, the trees, the deer, and the bears. Perhaps in the caverns beneath Knoxville there dwelt the grandfather of all bears—a spiritual changeling that could appear as both a bear and a man. Perhaps it still dwells there to this day.

The Ghosts of UTK

There is hardly a college campus on earth that does not sport at least one resident spook. In Johnson City the ghost of Sidney Gilbreath, the founding father of East Tennessee State University, haunts the hall named in his honor. At Virginia Intermont in Bristol, the supposed ghost of Vera Tepes haunts an old burned out room. (A few years ago, however, we discovered to our chagrin that Vera was alive and well and living in Texas. But what the hey, a legend is a legend— right?) At Sweet Briar, Virginia, the ghost of Daisy Williams roams the Sweet Briar College campus at will.

The University of Tennessee boasts a multitude of ghosts. For instance, the ghosts of Union soldiers are said to haunt "The Hill" near Neyland Stadium. The ghost of Sophronia Strong haunts the residence hall named in her honor. The ghost of the former director of the Hoskins Library haunts that building's dark corners.

Another Hoskins Library ghost is called the "Evening Primrose." She is blamed for unexplained footsteps in the building, elevators mysteriously moving from floor to floor, books falling off the shelves by themselves, and the odor of baking corn bread wafting through the building. Whenever the corn bread was detected, it was assumed that the Evening Primrose was preparing her supper.

The ghosts of Native Americans are said to haunt the Agriculture Campus. An Archaic Indian mound (not Cherokee, however) is located there.

Former UT dean of education John A. Thackston is said to haunt the headquarters of the General Counseling Center on Lake Avenue. The ghost of Thackston, who built the house, walks its halls, opening and closing doors.

UNQUIET SHADOWS
The period just after the War Between the States saw tremendous physical growth of the UT campus, as this 1890s photograph of "The Hill" plainly shows. Unfortunately part of the campus had been used to bury Union soldiers, but the locations of their graves were unknown. After the flurry of construction, "The Hill" suddenly became rife with ghosts. Later, the bones of some of the fallen soldiers were discovered beneath the structures of the most haunted "houses" on campus.

Perhaps one of the main reasons for all this supernatural activity is because UT has such a long history, going back to even before Tennessee became a state. And perhaps, like any large university, UT has suffered more than its share of unique personalities. Take the case of Stephan Foster, a Presbyterian minister and physics professor who tried to bring a dead man back to life.

The first electrochemical battery was documented by Alessandro Volta in a letter to the Royal Society of London in 1800. Almost immediately, European scientists began to wonder whether this newly harnessed energy might be used to bring the dead back to life. So they began hooking electrodes up to all sorts of deceased animals and got the shock of their lives when charges sent into the dismembered leg of a dead frog, for example, caused it to kick.

Mary Wollstonecraft Shelley, daughter of political philosopher William Godwin and women's rights advocate Mary

Wollstonecraft, and second wife of the poet Percy Bysshe Shelley, is famous as the author of *Frankenstein, or The Modern Prometheus* (1818), a novel whose popularity as a horror tale has, unfortunately, eclipsed its deep philosophical content. The story concerns a medical student, Victor Frankenstein, who learns how to resurrect dead flesh. Thus he creates a nameless monster who is physically ugly but innately good. But the monster turns evil when Frankenstein refuses to accept and nurture him. After the monster kills Frankenstein's bride and brother, the scientist pursues him to the North Pole, where they both perish. The book became a runaway best-seller and fired the public's imagination, including that of the Reverend Mr. Foster's.

Foster had come to East Tennessee College (as UT was known then) as a protégé of the Reverend Charles Coffin, former president of Greeneville College, who was appointed president of ETC in 1826. Foster's salary was $600 per year and he supplemented his income by pastoring at the Second Presbyterian Church in Knoxville. It was this church that Foster turned into his own "Frankenstein's laboratory" for his grand experiment.

One has to wonder about the mind-set of the college, the church, the community, and the government of Knox County, when Professor Foster proposed his unique little exploit into the realm of the creation (or re-creation, if you prefer) of life. If President Coffin had any qualms about his physics professor's bizarre experiment, he kept his peace. Coffin was known to be generally supportive of new ideas. Yet this was an era when the very idea of the creation of life was left exclusively to God. It was a wonder, considering the events soon to transpire, that the good professor escaped a hasty lynching by an ecclesiastically offended mob. Instead, they cheered him on.

Foster started the ball rolling by asking Knox County officials for access to the next executed prisoner. Then, while he waited, he busied himself constructing a number of batteries. (Commercial batteries were not available until much later.) Finally the city of Knoxville provided a body, that of a young man who had killed his wife's lover. Foster had the corpse carried inside the Second Presbyterian Church where he had set up his experiment. Then, while a crowd of Knoxvillians gawked through the church windows, Foster set electrical current surging through the body. According to one witness, the body convulsed and the chest heaved three times as if it were breathing. Then nothing.

The experiment was over—for all intents and purposes a failure. Yet the people of Knoxville didn't see it that way. They gave the professor a hearty cheer because they believed that he was well on the road to conquering death!

When the Reverend Stephan Foster conducted his experiment in 1829, East Tennessee College was barely thirty-five years old. Chartered by the Territorial Legislature in 1794 as Blount College (named for territorial governor William Blount), the school began in a two-story frame building on the corner of Gay and Clinch streets. Tuition was $8.00 for each session of five months, and board was $25.00. Its only president/teacher was the Reverend Samuel Czare Carrick. But even in its first years of existence, the college was unique. Among the students were five women, including Barbara Blount, daughter of Governor Blount himself. For this reason Blount College is considered the first coeducational college in America.

Pretty, blonde Barbara Blount, as well as the other four women enrolled in the school—Polly McClung, Jenny Armstrong, and sisters Mattie and Kitty Kain—had dormitories named in their honor. We can only assume that four of the dorms were erected without incident. The construction of Barbara Blount Hall, however, liberated a legion of Union ghosts looking for their bodies.

A former resident of Blount Hall told me that one time she saw at least a half dozen ghosts of Union soldiers on the first floor of the building. "They were wandering around aimlessly," she said. "They took no notice of me, but I was petrified. I stood right where I was until they disappeared through a wall."

The ghosts of Barbara Blount Hall were, of course, shadows of an earlier time, and their origin can be traced back to an incident that took place during the siege of Knoxville. Fort Sanders was a Union earthwork on a hill west of Knoxville. On November 29, 1863, Confederate General James Longstreet launched an attack against the fort. The Confederates charged up the hill but got tangled up in an almost invisible web of telegraph wire strung from stump to stump. Some of the men tripped and fell into a ditch surrounding the fort.

The ditch was steep and about twenty feet deep. At the bottom the Confederates found themselves facing a nearly perpendicular wall sheathed in ice. Union infantrymen fired their muskets into the hordes of trapped Confederates. Artillerists shortened the fuses on their shells and dropped them into the ditch. The Confederates could do nothing but surrender or be massacred.

The battle lasted twenty minutes. Longstreet lost over 800 men, Burnside only thirteen.

During the construction of Barbara Blount Hall in 1901, workmen's shovels struck a wooden box buried in the dirt. The box turned out to be a coffin containing the bones and half-rotted uniform of a Union soldier. Seven more coffins were recovered containing a like number of Burnside's troops killed at the Battle of Fort Sanders thirty-eight years before. Historian Betsey Creekmore said that the bodies were removed and reburied at Knoxville's National Cemetery in unmarked graves.

That should have been the end of the story, but it wasn't. Campus legend says that the bodies might have been removed, but the souls of the men stayed put where they were. When Barbara Blount Hall was completed, the ghosts of the soldiers in uniform roamed the halls in the lower part of the building looking for their bodies. Since Blount Hall was a female dormitory, one can only wonder how many of the stories about the haunting are about real experiences or the result of practical jokes played by boys at the expense of the girls.

One story concerns a college junior who was cuddled up

all snug under the covers one frosty winter's night when she had the sudden feeling that someone was watching her. She opened her eyes and saw a man standing at the foot of her bed looking down at her. He was tall and gaunt, wore a Civil War uniform, and his eyes were like fire. The girl screamed and the ghost disappeared.

Was this a prank? Not likely. Security in the old Barbara Blount Hall was legendary. (One defender of female honor, an elderly matron who guarded the door like a wizened but ferocious troll, was jokingly said to have been offered the job of chief of security when work first began on the atomic bomb at nearby Oak Ridge.) It is highly improbable that any impish lad had managed to gain entry to the building, much less escaped without a trace after the fact.

Barbara Blount Hall was torn down in 1979, a relic of an earlier day that had outlived its usefulness. Now the place

Courtesy of the Library of Congress

SOMETHING WALKS IN BARBARA BLOUNT HALL
When Barbara Blount Hall was built in 1901, workmen found seven coffins containing the remains of Union soldiers killed at the battle of nearby Fort Saunders. The bodies were removed, but apparently, the spirits remained. Ghosts bedeviled the female residents of the dormitory until the old building was finally torn down to make way for a parking lot.

THE HILL OF DISRUPTED DREAMS
During the War Between the States, Knoxville, like many other cities in the South, was an armed camp whose occupation forces changed with the tides of war. This wet-plate photograph was taken during the period of Union occupation. The Tennessee River is in the middle background with the buildings of UT just dimly visible on the hill beyond. At the time, the school had suspended classes and was being used as a hospital. Most of its male students were either at war or had been killed on the battlefield. It would not be until after Appomattox that UT would resume operation.

where this fine old structure stood is covered with a parking lot—an eternal monument to the ever increasing number of automobiles on campus. Some say that the ghosts departed when the building was razed. Others are not too sure. At least, there have not been any recent sightings of apparitions in the immediate vicinity.

Other Union soldiers, presumably from the same Battle of Fort Sanders, are said to haunt an apartment house on the corner of Laurel Avenue and 15th Street. Residents reported seeing odd figures moving around the grounds in the daylight and experienced bizarre happenings at night. When an expert was called in to investigate, he said that the house was, indeed, haunted. Could the remaining five Union casualties, who were not found in the excavation for Barbara Blount Hall, be buried beneath that apartment house?

Who was (is) Sophronia Marrs Strong? Certainly she is not the goddess of war as her maiden name suggests. In fact Sophie, as she is affectionately known, is a person (ghost) who looks out for students whom she considers her children. In that department, at least, Sophie has had plenty of experience.

Sophie was born in 1817 in nearby Shelbyville. She married Dr. Joseph C. Strong, a Knoxville physician, when she was about sixteen years old. Then she took up residence in the doctor's fine brick home (built in 1804, it was the first one of that material to have been erected in the city), where she commenced to bear children—twelve in all. She died in 1867 at the age of fifty. In the 1890s the Strong house, located at State Street and Cumberland Avenue, became one of the first hospitals in Knoxville. The house was later torn down to make way for new construction at UTK.

In 1915 one of Sophie's sons, Benjamin Rush Strong, willed property to UT to build Strong Hall. He put two conditions on the gift. First, Strong Hall would be a female dormitory. The second condition was that a wildflower garden would always be maintained outside.

Managing so many of her own children during her life must have convinced Sophie to carry on after her death. The first unit of Strong Hall was completed in 1923—launching Sophie's second career, as ghostly caretaker of UT students. Yvonne Loveday wrote that "students claim Sophie's spirit remains at Strong Hall to lead them on the path of proper living." Her ghost appears as a "lady in white" whose image appears in a mirror on her birthday—February 17.

Apparently she is a playful sprite who likes to pull pranks on the students. Sometimes she locks students out of their rooms, for what reason no one seems to know. Worse still, in a woman's dormitory at least, bathroom doors are mysteriously locked when no one occupies them. Also, mysterious lights appear out of nowhere and float lazily down the corridors, prompting whoever is wandering the hall at the moment to flee into her room and bolt the door behind her.

Sophie has little patience with arguing and fighting among her "children." One fast way to summon her ghost is for a discussion to get rowdy. One day two young ladies began to discuss a current issue. Unfortunately, these lasses were a bit hot tempered, and debate turned into argument, and argument turned into a shouting match. In the midst of this verbal free-for-all, one of the girls suddenly fell silent. Her opponent was quite convinced that she had won the battle until she took note of the expression on the girl's face, staring in horror at something straight ahead. Her adversary turned around and was shocked to see the ghost of Sophie, hands on her hips, glaring disapprovingly at the combatants!

Another ghost of UTK is that of a solemn young man whose apparition plods the road that runs by the former site of Jefferson Hall, a relatively new building, only ten years old when it was destroyed by fire in 1934. He wears old-fashioned clothing—a celluloid collar and bowler hat. He walks with his head bent and his hands behind his back, as if in deep thought.

The story behind this ghost is that the young man, once a student, was very unlucky in love. He had been dating a young lady and was intending to marry her, when she suddenly ran off to Boston to wed another. The boy lived in a state of despair for several weeks. Then, according to tradition, he took a pistol and blew out his brains. The story goes on to say that if the apparition ever took off his hat, a huge gaping wound would be visible in the side of his head.

This ghost apparently takes no notice of living beings around him, as one young lady found out when going to class one day. As she walked along, a figure fell into step beside her. From his costume she reckoned he was a member of a campus drama troupe. When she turned to ask him what play he was in, she noticed that she could see right through the figure!

Old Science Hall on campus was razed in 1967, felled in the name of progress. But while it stood, Science Hall was the pride of the campus. Built in 1894 at a cost of about $40,000, it was not so much a beautiful building as it was architecturally interesting. It had a tower, a balcony, and rounded arches. Inside there were high ceilings, a small auditorium, and a pipe organ. The auditorium, while doubling for a chapel, also played host to numerous dramatic and musical performances.

One former thespian, known only as Fanny, haunted the old auditorium and was even seen roaming the corridors of the building. So far there is no explanation of how Fanny died, although some think it was from tuberculosis. It is generally agreed on, however, that Fanny loved the theater and wanted to make acting her career. She was excellent at pantomime, and when a movie company shot a film in Knoxville in the 1920s, Fanny was first in line for local auditions. She won a small part and it is believed that the producers were so

Courtesy of the Library of Congress

THE HAUNTED BUILDING THAT USED TO BE
The old Science Hall, demolished in 1967, was the home of the ghost of a young UT student who desperately wanted to be an actress. But she died suddenly, just before she was to go to Hollywood to appear in silent pictures.

impressed with her performance that they offered her a contract to come to Hollywood to act in the flickers. The unfortunate Fanny then fell ill and died a year later.

Our last UT ghost is a barghest. In English folklore, a barghest is a monstrous dog with huge claws and teeth. This creature is said to roam around Yorkshire, and anyone who sees the dog will die soon after.

There are barghests reported in Tennessee. On the grounds of Rotherwood Mansion in Kingsport, a monstrous black dog is said to roam, howling mournfully. Locally, he's called "Hound of Hell." Again, anyone who sees this creature is certain to suffer imminent death.

In Wales, a barghest is called a "Gwyligi," or "Dog of Darkness." On the Isle of Man, it is called "Mauthe Doog." At UTK, it's called "Scary"!

UTK's barghest lurks in the vicinity of "The Hill" and, on moonlit nights, emits a low mournful howl that sounds like a baying wolf. There was a time that complaints about the noisy animal would send security scurrying to chase the animal. No more.

The tale that I heard was that one night the howling of the animal was especially loud and mournful. Two officers were immediately dispatched to investigate and saw a large dog—much larger than normal—sitting on the hill. The officers drew their pistols and cautiously approached the animal. The dog was large enough that he could have made short work of the officers if he had chosen to attack. But, for some reason, he was either unaware of their advance or ignoring them.

When the officers were about fifty feet away, they paused for a moment. Perhaps they were trying to decide whether to simply shoot the animal or take the chance that he was friendly enough to coax into the back of their prowl car and haul off to the animal shelter. Its size intimidated them to be sure, but still....

One of the officers said, "Hello, boy," in a low, soothing voice.

The dog suddenly turned. The officers froze in terror. The

dog's eyes were glowing with an eerie ruby red light. Then it bared its long, white fangs, drooling with saliva. To hear some of the students tell the story, security on the hill was suddenly left unsecured as the two officers hightailed it for their car, jumped in, and sped away in a cloud of screeching rubber and a spray of cinders.

Photo by the Author

LINGERING MEMORY
Most of the classic haunted buildings of the UT campus have given way to more modern structures. But ghosts, like people, can adapt to new surroundings. In spite of inhabiting one of the most modern campuses in Tennessee, the ghosts of UTK—as well as their legend—*live* on.

Unhappy Spirits

In a day when wall-to-wall carpeting covers the floors of many houses, it is uncommon to see a home sporting bare wooden floors. There are, however, notable exceptions—especially in historic houses.

Mrs. P. of Kingston Pike owns a very old house that was built sometime just before the War Between the States. The original wide-plank floors still in the house are kept in a state of high polish and are very beautiful. Only one scatter rug is in the house, in the dining room. It looks so out of place that a person is tempted to ask why it is there.

The reason the rug is there is a very good one. There is a disturbing face etched in the floor beneath it!

When the rug is removed, the face is clearly visible in the grain of the wood. It is the face of a man who looks as though he is in terrible agony. It could have been a fluke of nature that such an image appeared in the wood at that place, except for one small detail. The figure extends past the edge of the board and over into the next. The odds of that happening are too overwhelming to calculate.

Mrs. P., who is not a superstitious woman, says that just after the house was built it was commandeered by Union occupation forces in Knoxville and used as a hospital. She believes that the image is of one of the soldiers who was in so much agony from his wounds that he fell off his cot. He hit the floor face down and his terrible agony was etched into the wood for all time.

"Several years ago," she said, "my husband and I completely refinished this floor. We thought that a thorough sanding would get rid of the face. But it didn't. Now we just throw a rug over that part of the floor and try to forget what

THE HAUNTED MONUMENT
John Sevier, early settler, soldier, Indian fighter, and first governor of Tennessee, died in 1815 while on a mission to Alabama. Seventy years later, his body was returned to Tennessee and laid to rest in its native soil. At the courthouse, a monument was construction to his memory, and wouldn't you just know it, the shade of Sevier has sometimes been reported to loiter around its base.

is underneath it."

According to popular mythology, mobile homes are considered to be a magnet for whirling tornadoes. If a tornado springs up, folks say it pauses for a moment to look around the countryside. Then the moment that it spots a mobile home in the immediate vicinity it roars straight for it—with predictable results.

Another mythology is that mobile homes are never haunted—blown down by ill winds, yes; infested by ghosts, no. Mobile homes just do not fill the mold of a classic haunted house. The popular concept of a haunted house is an old run-down structure, abused by neglect, time, and the weather. But try to tell that to Laura M., a thirtyish single mother who lives in East Knoxville. She swears that her mobile home is haunted by a very unhappy spirit. It gives everyone who hears it, including herself, the willies.

"It cries all the time," Laura told me. "It's the saddest, most forlorn sound that I've ever heard. At night the sobs echo through the house. It sounds like someone's poor old heart is breaking. Sometimes I feel like I want to cry right along with it."

I asked her if the ghost frightened her.

"Not so much frighten," she replied nervously. "More like I feel uneasy when it's around. You know, it's that supernatural thing—the fear of the unknown. Raises goose bumps on me when I hear it crying. My kids, on the other hand, consider a ghost in the house as cool. They're quite happy with it around. My oldest girl—she's twelve—has got a lot of friends at school that know about the ghost, and they like to come for a sleep over to hear the ghost. There's someone here every weekend it seems. And, of course, our house is every popular around Halloween. Sometimes my daughter has four or five little girls at once for sleep overs about the end of October.

"My youngest—he's ten—and he's at that age when everything is 'cool' or 'awesome.' But he sure learned the hard way about 'cool' ghosts. One night I had to go over to a neighbor's house for something or other. Bobby was glued to the TV, so since I wouldn't be so far away and I would be coming right back, I decided to leave him where he was.

"Five minutes later there was a knock on the neighbor's door and when she answered it, there was Bobby. He was scared to death. 'Mom,' he cried, 'that ghost is in the house again!' He never wanted to stay there alone by himself again."

"Did you ever see the ghost?" I asked Laura.

"I never did, but my daughter claims that she did—or, thought that she did. As I said, she has a lot of her little friends overnight and they wait in bed—all shivery and stuff—waiting to hear the ghost. One night, about two months ago, the ghost started up again at about one in the morning. My daughter and a friend had just gotten to sleep and the noise woke them up. I was in my own bed reading when the crying started.

"Suddenly I heard screaming, and both little girls burst into my room. Their eyes were wide like saucers. They literally flew into my bed and buried themselves underneath the covers.

"'We saw it, Mommy,' my daughter said, the thick blankets muffling her voice. 'It's in my bedroom!'

"When I finally got the girls calmed down, we all went for a look and, of course, didn't see a thing. I asked them what the ghost looked like. My daughter said it was like a white shadow that floated across the room. Although she couldn't see the face clearly, she said that she was sure it was a woman."

Laura then told me that one of her neighbors said the trailer was once inhabited by a young couple who had just gotten married. The man died in an automobile accident about a month later and his wife was inconsolable. She literally stopped living and wasted away to nothing. In spite of all attempts to reach her, she literally died of a broken heart. She was found later by a clergyman who had come by to check up on her. It is said that it is her ghost that is heard sobbing though the house.

"You know," Laura said, "the kids get along better with our ghosts than do adults."

"What do you mean?" I asked.

"I'm still young," she answered, "and not bad looking."

I agreed.

"My husband and I were divorced several years ago and I think I'd like to get involved with someone else. It's lonely and hard being a single mother. But I'm afraid to invite anyone over here.

"About six months ago I met a man, about a year younger than me, and we hit it right off. I thought that the relationship could really go somewhere. He had a good job and my kids liked him. He was also quite handsome. We all went to the Knoxville Zoo for a picnic one day and really had a good time. So one night I decided to cook dinner—you know—to demonstrate my domestic skills."

She paused to chuckle, then continued.

"I fixed a really nice meal—roast beef, browned potatoes, corn, hot rolls, apple pie—lots of the fat and carbohydrates that men like. I spent most of the day preparing dinner—it was Saturday—and, for once, everything turned out perfect.

"Later on, after I had sent the kids to bed, we were sitting on the couch watching a video. Then the ghost showed up. There was all this crying and my friend jumped up off the couch like he had been burned.

"'It's true,' he shouted. 'This place really is haunted!'

"'How did you know?' I asked. 'I never told you about my ghost.'

"'Laura,' he said, 'This place is infamous. But I didn't believe it. I might as well tell you right now, I don't like ghosts!'

"With that he threw on his coat and ran out the door. And as soon as he started his car and drove away, the crying stopped.

"The next day, I saw my friend. He had this sheepish look on his face. He apologized for running out like that but said that he didn't think our relationship was going anywhere and that it would be best if we didn't see each other again socially. I could tell he was lying through his teeth, but there was nothing that I could do about it."

The crying ghost still haunts Laura and her family. For a time she thought she would try to get a preacher to exorcise the spook but, so far, has had no luck in finding a volunteer. She also thought about moving away and leaving the ghost to the next tenant. But she rejected that idea, too. She likes her neighbors, and the mobile home is convenient to schools and shopping.

So she has resolved herself to her fate—hosting a house ghost that has overstayed her welcome but apparently has no intention of leaving.

I'm sorry that our ghost didn't perform for you," Laura said as I was leaving. "Mainly we hear it at night—almost never during the day."

I nodded.

"You seem to be the kind of gentleman who wouldn't be afraid of her," she added. Then she smiled. "You're not looking for a wife, are you?"

She seemed disappointed when I told her that I was happily married.

"Oh, well," she sighed. "Maybe someday I'll find someone who can live with both me and my ghost."

She closed the door and I walked to my car. As I was pulling away, the school bus was just pulling up. A pretty little girl and her brother ran across the road and past my car. As they went by, the girl gave me a fleeting glance—perhaps wondering what I was doing there. Then they ran inside the trailer and the door slammed shut behind them.

That is quite a household, I thought to myself. *One lonely woman, two bright kids, and a sorrowful, crying ghost.* As the old saying goes, it's an interesting place to visit but I wouldn't want to live there.

The Haunted Bottle

For a number of years now there has been a frenzy of bottle collecting in this country. Not the plastic kind of bottle that now sits on grocers' shelves, but bottles—real glass bottles—the kind that bear no marks of mass production on them.

There was a time, not too long ago, when most glass bottles were made by hand. Only after the turn of the twentieth century were bottles generally mass produced. Although most all looked the same, each handmade bottle was slightly different. There were medicine bottles, whiskey bottles, bottles with long necks, bottles with short necks—every possible shape and size. Now collectors wash 'em up, clean 'em up, and display 'em on the mantle or in the den. Handmade bottles are even considered by some to be works of art. And a rare bottle, in reasonably good shape, can command big bucks!

If we go back in time we find that many unusual substances came in glass bottles—bitters, poisons, snake oil, and even ghosts. Yes, that's right. I said ghosts. It is a well-known fact that ghosts generally haunt houses or other large structures. But is it possible that a ghost could haunt a simple object like a bottle?

Manabee is a term used in the East Tennessee mountains to describe a ghost that haunts a small object. It could be an article of clothing, a gun (as in one story from Unicoi County), a car, or a bottle. Like Mary's little lamb, everywhere the object went, the ghost was sure to go.

Manabee hauntings are more common than one would imagine. I heard a story a few years ago about a Knoxville antique collector who purchased a strange-looking bottle in a secondhand shop. It looked old, very old. So she bought the object and took it home. For the few pennies that she spent, she thought she was getting a very unusual buy. But, as she quickly discovered, unusual was an understatement.

Almost immediately, odd things began to happen. For one thing, the bottle would never stay where she put it. When she placed it on her mantle, a few hours later she would find the bottle on an end table. If she placed the bottle on an end table, she would later find it perched on the mantle. This was rather bizarre, because the woman lived alone.

Then came the crashing sounds. Late at night she would hear the sound of glass breaking, as if something had fallen to the floor and had shattered into a million pieces. When she ran downstairs to investigate, she would find her strange bottle lying on the floor, intact. A further search of the house turned up no broken glass. This happened several times.

Two weeks after she brought her bottle home, events really got spooky. She awoke one night with the distinct feeling that she was being watched. She opened her eyes and saw the shadow of a man standing at the foot of her bed. Naturally she screamed bloody murder. The apparition disappeared. A moment later she found the bottle, resting on the floor in the exact same spot where the figure had been standing! The last time she had seen it, the bottle was sitting on a table in her den downstairs. How could it have gotten upstairs?

At this point the woman resolved that she had had enough of her rambling, ghostly bottle and decided she would return it to the secondhand dealer for a refund. When she approached the counter, bottle in hand, the man got a funny look on his face.

"I would like to return this bottle, sir," she said. Then she lied to avoid telling him her strange story and being laughed at. "I found, when I got home, that I already had one just like it."

The shop owner knew better. "No ma'am," he replied. "You do not have another bottle like that one. Nobody has a bottle like that."

"What do you mean?" the woman asked, somewhat in a huff.

"I have tried to get rid of that horrible thing for years," he replied calmly. "Why do you think that I sold you such a valuable antique so cheap? There's something not right with that thing, and everybody who has bought it knows it. That bottle comes with a ghost."

"How do you know that?" the woman demanded.

"I have seen the ghost with my own eyes, madam, as I am sure that you have. Otherwise you would not be trying to return the bottle to me. There is the figure of a man in old-fashioned clothing. Wherever that bottle goes, so does the ghost. I think I have sold that bottle a dozen times, and every time it comes back to me. The customer sees the ghost and is scared to death. And I accept the bottle and hand over a refund. Well, enough is enough. I will not accept that bottle from you. You bought it and it's yours, spook and all!"

So that was that. The first thought the woman had upon leaving the shop was to dump the bottle into the nearest trash can, which she did. But when she walked in the door of her house, she was shocked to discover the bottle—as big as life—sitting on her living room mantle. This would never do. She was determined that she was not going to be haunted by a bottle for the rest of her life. But how could she get rid of it?

Maybe she should break it to smithereens. So she took the bottle to her garage, wrapped it in a thick piece of cloth to protect herself from flying glass, placed it on the workbench, grabbed a nearby claw hammer, and brought the tool down sharply. The hammer's head glanced off the bottle. She hit it again. Still no effect. She unwrapped the bottle and found there was no damage, not even a chip in the glass. For an hour she tried to break that bottle, but to no avail. Finally she gave up.

She couldn't "lose" the bottle and she couldn't destroy it. Maybe if she could discover a little about its history she could discover the nature of her ghost, and then find a way to exorcise it. The owner of the secondhand shop where she had bought the bottle was no help. He had purchased it in a large cardboard box filled with other bottles at an estate sale.

Finally she decided to ask an expert. The woman was acquainted with a man who collected old bottles as a hobby.

"That's easy," he said brightly. "This is an old whiskey bottle. The label is worn off but this is definitely an old whiskey bottle."

"Would you like to buy it?" the woman asked hopefully.

"Not likely," he replied. "There are a lot of these bottles around. I have two of them myself. They're not very valuable. Too many of them around."

The woman drew a deep breath and the collector handed the haunted bottle back to her. "Then, sir, could you tell me if anything funny has happened to you with the bottles you own?"

The man raised his eyebrows and looked at her suspiciously. "Just what do you mean by 'funny'?"

The woman decided not to push her inquiry further. Instead, she turned and walked away, resigned to the fact that she was stuck with her haunted bottle.

Years passed. The ghost appeared often, always at the foot of the woman's bed. Glass crashed, but no shards were ever found. And the bottle would move from place to place around her house, apparently under its own power. But now she was getting used to the ghostly goings-on. Then one day a friend was visiting. She saw the bottle and inquired about it. "Would you like to sell it to me?" the friend asked.

The woman thought about it for a moment. Now was her chance to rid herself of the infernal thing. And why should she tell her friend about the ghost that was attached to it? Why not let her find out for herself.

"How much are you offering?" she asked.

Her friend told her.

She was about to say all right, but a powerful twinge of guilt suddenly tugged at her. *Sell my bottle?* she asked herself. *After all we've been through together? What would my ghost do without me?*

To her immense surprise, she found herself refusing the offer that she had so long prayed for. In fact, she had quite a few offers after that one, and she refused each and every one.

She couldn't bear to part with her ghost. He was actually company in her lonely house. And the bottle—ghost and all—has been in her family ever since.

Things That Go Bump in the Night

A poltergeist is a ghost that announces its presence by noises, rappings, and the creation of general disorder. One seldom sees an actual apparition, and for many, that is the really creepy part of a poltergeist haunting. Perhaps if we knew what was actually creating the noises, we would be less afraid—even if we knew for certain that the culprit was as dead as a doornail. Here is a case in point:

Todd lives in a split-level house, located in north Knoxville. He said the house was built sometime in the 1950s. The previous owner had a son who had been involved in a very bad car accident and suffered a massive head injury. Eventually he died, and Todd believes that it is his ghost that haunts the house. Although not a very actively haunted house (in the classic sense of the word), there have been two occasions that make Todd believe that there is something very odd going on.

One time he and his father were sitting in the den when they both heard the front door open, then slam shut. Then came sounds of footsteps walking up the stairs (which were located right next to the den). Then came the sound of the opening and shutting of the bedroom door. Todd thought that his mother had come home, but when he went upstairs to talk to her, she was not there. There was no one else in the house except Todd and his father. Yet the noises that they both had heard were distinct—unmistakable

The second strange event concerned a desk lamp. It was the kind that would turn on when someone touched it. There are three different positions of light intensity—a person touches the lamp one, two, or three times. There have been times when the lamp was turned to the first position and, then, increased or decreased in brightness of its own accord.

At first Todd thought that there might be something wrong with the lamp. Then one day, when the lamp was off, Todd heard three distinct clicks (although there is normally no sound) and the lamp turned itself on to the highest brilliance. There was no one else around the lamp at the time. "It scared the bejeebers out of me," Todd said. He added that this has happened only once, but once was enough. He has never forgotten the experience.

The ghosts of the Baker-Peters House can be classified as poltergeists—so can the piano-playing spirit described in "The Quick, the Dead, and the Quickly Dead" chapter later in this book. In fact, the greatest majority of hauntings are poltergeist hauntings. Many times strange noises, especially in old buildings, are passed over, attributed to natural pops and creaks of the aging structure. Sudden fluctuations in the brilliance of an electric lamp may be blamed on power surges or wiring problems. Even mysterious voices, coming out of nowhere, sometimes have a very logical explanation. Metal fillings in teeth, for example, sometimes pick up radio waves, and the person's mouth can act as a crude receiver. In cases like this it is entirely possible that a person's dental work will broadcast the Top 40.

However, some unexplained noises cannot be brushed off so easily. There is the tale of a little girl who kept hearing the sound of a crying child coming from her closet. (Her mouth, by the way, was completely devoid of fillings.)

Her parents, of course, thought their daughter's active imagination was the culprit—that is until they discovered that several years earlier the house had been occupied by a family whose little girl was literally starved to death while locked up in that very closet. The poor girl's parents were convicted of her death and were now guests of the state's penal system. Still, that did not stop the ghostly crying in the closet. Everyone in the house eventually heard it, and the unearthly sound was giving them the creeps.

The wife of the present owner was a compassionate woman who thought that the ghost might be lonely. Her own little girl refused to stay—much less sleep—in the room, so she decided that she would try to pacify the ghost until it could be decided what to do about it. She went to the local toy store and bought a huge stuffed teddy bear. "This is your bear," she said softly as she placed the overstuffed toy in the closet. "Have fun," she added as she shut the door.

The ploy worked, because the crying stopped. Eventually the woman found an open-minded cleric who laid hands on the closet and, allegedly, released the spirit of the little girl from its earthbound plane. The ghost was heard from no more, and the woman's own daughter ultimately returned to the room.

Some folks who study this kind of phenomenon on a scientific basis contend that poltergeist hauntings most often occur in houses where a pre-pubescent child is present. They think that hormones which begin surging just prior to puberty exude a mysterious force that causes ashtrays to fly off tables and crockery to be hurled around the room.

I have no doubt, being a parent myself, that the average twelve-year-old has countless emotional crosses to bear. But, at the same time, I have difficulty believing that little Jaimie in the following tale was the sole cause of Great Aunt Edna's portrait suddenly dangling six feet in midair without the benefit of human hands.

Jaimie's mother admits that when Jaimie reached the mystical age of twelve, her demeanor took a genuine turn for the worse. Almost overnight she turned from a bright, happy child into a sullen, argumentative lass whose apparent goal in life was to drive her parents crazy. In other words, a typical preteen-ager. Her mother chalked up the change to too much MTV, so she unplugged the television set and suggested that Jaimie go outside and soak up some healthful East Tennessee sunshine. Predictably Jaimie rebelled. It was not long before strange things began happening.

The "haunting" began subtly. Jaimie's mother would put something on a table one minute, only to find it gone the next. When she asked her daughter about the object (one day it happened to be a valuable diamond ring), the child pleaded innocent.

One time Jaimie's father "misplaced" a heavy Craftsman toolbox. After placing it on his workbench in the garage, he went inside to eat lunch, and found it gone when he returned. He searched everywhere but could not find it. Finally he decided that thieves had crept into the garage while he was enjoying his bowl of Campbell's soup and heisted his valuable tools. So he called the cops. They arrived and immediately found the missing object resting comfortably underneath the bench—in the very spot that Jaimie's father had looked a dozen times before. Needless to say, the man was totally embarrassed. Once again, little Jaimie had no knowledge of the mysterious disappearance/appearance of the bright red toolbox.

Great Aunt Edna belonged to the mother's side of the family. She was known to be a cantankerous old matriarch with so much money in the bank that she could live in luxury off the interest. Of course, everyone in the family suffered silently in the face of Great Aunt Edna's considerable litany of eccentricities while they cast greedy eyes towards the aged crone's hefty bankroll. Whenever she died (if she ever would), they aimed to inherit their fair share of her fortune.

One morning Great Aunt Edna was, indeed, found dead on the bathroom floor. After a well-attended funeral that dished out more than the usual portion of wailing and gnashing of teeth, the bereaved family members met in the lawyer's office to divvy up the estate. Some got considerable amounts of money. Some inherited real estate. Jaimie's mother, who had spent a great deal of time caring for the old woman in her later years, got the oil painting.

Disappointed? Yes. Bitter? Well, maybe just a little. In any event, Jaimie's mother toted the oversized oil home. Her practical husband figured that the heavy gold-leafed frame, at least, might be worth a few dollars. But instead of selling it, she talked her husband into hanging Great Aunt Edna over the fireplace.

Several years later, strange things began occurring in the house. The mother and father blamed Jaimie for objects that would mysteriously turn up missing, but the girl always pleaded innocent. The mother had read that young children were often inadvertently to blame for poltergeist activity, and she prayed that her daughter would reach puberty quickly so that the family could finally have some peace.

Then one day the mother walked into the living room and saw the massive portrait of Great Aunt Edna hovering in the middle of the room, about five or six feet off the floor. And there was nothing holding it up but air! The woman screamed and the portrait immediately plunged to the floor, the ancient gold-leafed frame cracking at the joints and the painting, itself, popping out of the frame. The husband came running.

"What happened?" he shouted.

"That picture was just hanging in midair," his wife replied with more than a hint of hysterics in her voice. "I screamed and it fell and broke."

The man walked over to the broken frame and knelt down. "What are these papers?" he asked.

"They fell out of the back of the frame, I suppose," the wife answered as she carefully approached her husband.

He turned toward her, waving a fistful of official looking certificates. "These are bonds," he said. "Municipal bonds."

"Are they worth anything?"

"I don't know, but I'm sure going to find out!"

Well, he did find out. And they were worth plenty—almost a million dollars. Great Aunt Edna had a habit of stashing valuables around the house for safekeeping, then forgetting all about them. She must have put the bonds behind her portrait and then, over the years, lost all track of their whereabouts. Or did she?

Great Aunt Edna had many faults, but ingratitude was not one of them. Jaimie's mother had spent many a difficult hour taking care of the old woman, as I said. But the old lady was also an incurable prankster. Maybe she knew all along that the bonds were in the frame. She had willed the painting to Jaimie's mother, perhaps knowing that she would be initially disappointed at her share of the estate, but also realizing that she would eventually find the treasure.

And just maybe, when Jaimie's mother hung the portrait over the mantle, Great Aunt Edna took matters into her own hands—so to speak—and smashed the frame to reveal the financial portfolio lurking behind the oil.

So, now, you decide. Was the culprit behind the haunting little Jaimie? Or was it the ghost of Great Aunt Edna trying to attract attention? Or both?

Mysteries, like *New York Times* crossword puzzles, are best solved with an open mind. It seems like anything is possible in this world, including ghosts. The unexpected windfall was a fact, there is no doubt about that. Inheritance tax was paid on the bonds, and Great Aunt Edna's will clearly states that only Jaimie's mother was to receive the oil. How the bonds were discovered, however, is another matter entirely and one that we must accept (if we are to accept it at all) on faith. And, as we all know, faith and an open mind go together like little girls and poltergeists.

Knoxville's Haunted Theaters

Every theater has at least one ghost—some even have two or more. Stage spooks range from star-crossed thespians to stagehands killed when they fell from the flies. The Barter Theatre in Abingdon, Virginia, contains a formless shape that strikes fear by its very presence, and it caused no less an actor than Ernest Borgnine to flee the building in terror. Memorial Theater in Johnson City, Tennessee, features phantom footfalls across the stage, as well as the ghost of a former projectionist. Ghosts and theaters go hand in hand, like bread and butter or Laurel and Hardy. Big, cavernous, shadowy auditoriums are a spooky kind of place—plenty of room to lurk about the gloom.

Knoxville has two haunted theaters—the Tennessee and the Bijou. The Tennessee, of course, is the most famous of the two. The Bijou, however, is probably the most haunted— maybe because its history is more checkered.

Right now the Bijou is in the throes of extensive renovations. The sharp raps from workmen's hammers forever resound through the structure. The sound is enough to wake the dead, and it probably does. But apparently the ghosts of the Bijou contribute their share of the noise. Heavy footfalls and formidable thumps on the ceiling are but two sounds in a seemingly endless repertoire of unexplained racket that often echoes through the old theater.

Past experience has proven that extensive renovation has a curious effect on ghosts. In the town of Jonesborough for example, just 100 miles up the road in Washington County, the same kind of a situation exists. Jonesborough is slowly being restored, building by building. Residents complain that ghostly activity (every house in Jonesborough seems to be haunted) increases when extensive renovations are taking place. It's as if the dead resent changes or alterations in their resting places. The ghostly activity, however, often ceases when the new resident assures the annoyed spook that the building is actually being restored to its former splendor.

The Bijou is actually composed of two buildings. Built in 1817, the Lamar House, a hotel which fronts Gay Street, was first opened as the plush Knoxville Hotel. The 1,500-seat Bijou, constructed at the rear of the hotel, was officially opened in 1908 as a legitimate theater. It was later converted into a movie house but remained home to the Knoxville Symphony and the Knoxville Opera. By 1965, however, the once-grand Bijou was called the Bijou Art Theatre and was reduced to showing porno flicks—culture had fled the building long before. Worse still, the Lamar House was renamed the LaMarr Hotel and was turned into a glorified bordello, complete with hourly rates. Patrons would go see a skin flick at the Bijou "Art Theater," then visit the LaMarr Hotel for a taste of the real thing. Prostitution was alive and well on Gay Street.

An offended city, however, was determined to impose economic hardship on the world's oldest profession. Warrants, charges, and indictments for prostitution piled up at the LaMarr Hotel, and finally, the court ordered the place closed. Then insult was added to injury when the property owner—an aged woman who was apparently unaware of the shenanigans that had been going on in the building—donated the hotel to the Church Street Methodist Church. The Methodists lost no time in selling the flea-bitten old hotel. And in 1975, the theater, itself, was shuttered.

Unlike its neighbor down the street that opened as a Vaudeville house, the Tennessee Theater is a relic from the days when movie theaters were palaces of plaster and gilt. The Tennessee opened on October 1, 1928, barely a year after sound was added to the movies. All through the Great Depression the theater flourished. But then came television. And on its heels came the business exodus away from downtown and into the suburbs. Moviegoers were no longer interested in attending a movie in a lavish hall attended by footmen in uniform, especially if they had to park three blocks away. The prosperity of the postwar years had quelled their fantasies and had deadened their hocks. They now went to see their movies in theaters that were no more than plain, oblong boxes with a screen at one end and a projector at the other. And they were walking three blocks across crowded parking lots rather then three blocks down the city street.

The once-proud Bijou became the Bijou Art Theater and showed porno flicks in order to stay in business, but the Tennessee was able to save face until the end. It finally closed in 1977, still showing first-run movies.

For the first time in forty-nine years, downtown Knoxville was without a first-run theater. But thanks to some far-sighted folks, the Bijou and the Tennessee didn't remain fallow very long.

The first phoenix to rise from the ashes was the Bijou. In 1977, after a year of frenzied fund-raising, the creaking old theater was purchased for $275,000 by Knoxville Heritage Association. Then the Tennessee was resurrected by a UT economics professor as a revival house for old films. But the project was underfinanced, and the theater closed a short time later for nonpayment of the rent.

But today, in spite of a number of false starts, both the Tennessee and the Bijou are showpieces, monuments to a community that stubbornly refused to let the past slip through their fingers. History is as much a part of both theaters as ceiling joists and proscenium arches. And even though both theaters are operated by professional managers, ghosts rule the roost.

It is generally agreed that the Tennessee Theatre is the less haunted of the two, but ghostly events do occur there. During the time of its construction, so the story goes, a workman fell from the ceiling and was killed. It is his ghost that haunts the theater. Sounds range from footfalls to loud crashing sounds. There have even been reports that a white cloud shape is sometimes seen floating around the stage when the hall is empty.

"TRAMP, TRAMP, TRAMP..."
The Tennessee Theater, the first of the two Gay Street theaters to be completely renovated, has a healthy complement of phantoms ranging from a poltergeist with "lead feet" to a white, shapeless form that drifts around the stage when the old theater is empty.

The Bijou, however, is reputed to be the haunting place of many spirits—but first here's the tale of a mysterious creature. Several years ago the board of directors allotted $1,000 to a firm called Varmint Buster to rid the theater of rats and mice. They got all but one, a hard-boiled rodent that contractors nicknamed "Ratzilla." Ratzilla is apparently alive and well, and still on the loose.

The ghosts of the Bijou are pretty much unidentified. They may be the spirits of actors or actresses that once graced the Bijou stage, Ethel Barrymore, George M. Cohen, or Al Jolson among them. Or, perhaps, the ghosts could even be former prostitutes who once populated the old hotel. Only one spook has been tentatively identified—Union Colonel William P. Sanders.

Colonel Sanders was a Kentucky-born West Pointer whose father was a prosperous chicken farmer (no snickering, please), and whose family was firmly grounded in Southern

IN THE THROES OF RENOVATION
Since the formerly infamous Lamar House fronts the old Bijou Theater, there is no grand marquee facing Gay Street. In fact, the Bijou's main entrance is rather obtuse, unlike the theater's most notorious inhabitant—a seemingly immortal rodent which was dubbed "Ratzilla" by exasperated exterminators.

traditions. But when war broke out, he left the family's homestead for the North and joined the federal cavalry.

Just before General Ambrose E. Burnside began his march on Knoxville in 1863, he was stripped of his command of the IX Corps which was sent to Vicksburg. Now short on men, and not knowing what lay ahead of him in East Tennessee, he sent a brigade of 1,500 cavalry under Sanders to look the situation over. Sanders and his troopers did more, however, than merely send back intelligence. They raised havoc throughout East Tennessee, severing rebel communications and destroying a number of bridges along the Tennessee & Virginia Railroad. He credited his amazing success to the helpfulness of East Tennesseans who were for the most part pro-Union and who were breathlessly waiting for federal troops to march in and save them from the clutches of the Confederacy.

Burnside, of course, took Knoxville, but during the battle

Colonel Sanders was wounded in a skirmish on Kingston Pike. The Lamar House had been turned into a hospital, and Sanders was brought there where he died the next day. That was in Room 11—the bridal suite. Since that time, the ghost of Colonel Sanders is said to haunt the old hotel. In 1908, when part of the hotel was demolished to make way for the Bijou, his ghostly activities transferred to the theater.

The ghosts of the Bijou are known to be a happy lot. Anna Garber, writing in the old *Knoxville Journal*, recounts a tale by Robbie Link, then-assistant to the director, about the time that workmen were laboring on the stage in the wee hours of the morning. "Their tape recorder was blasting away, but between songs they heard 'laughing, hollering and running up and down stairs,' Link said. Several times they checked the area on the second floor from where the noise was coming, but found nothing. Finally the workmen 'got so weirded out [that] they left.'"

Link went on to say that most people weren't afraid of the ghosts. "My little boy thinks its fun," he said. "He's five. He loves to come here."

Photo by the Author

IT'S ENOUGH TO WAKE THE DEAD
A worker leaves the Bijou by the most convenient doorway from the auditorium—an emergency exit high above the street. The banging and clattering of workmen renovating the Bijou has awakened its ghosts—a happy-go-lucky band of spooks, apparently raising a little Cain of their own.

The Quick, the Dead, and the Quickly Dead

From Ireland comes the legend of the banshee, a demon in the form of a beautiful woman whose mournful cry foretells imminent death. From Kingsport, Tennessee, there is the story of the "Hound of Hell" that scampers through the underbrush surrounding Rotherwood Mansion, wailing in the dead of night. From the hills of Southwest Virginia there is the legend of Lullaby Aggie, the ghost of a woman who died in childbirth, who sings to her stillborn child.

Ghosts are not silent by any means. Many of them have a voice and they use it. One of the older houses in Knoxville, for example, was used as a temporary hospital during the War Between the States. To this day, if a person listens carefully, he can hear the cries and wails of the wounded who once suffered great pain within its walls.

Instances of noisy ghosts are more common than one would imagine. Numerous are the cries of anguish. Others are simply noises—banging, thumping sounds made by an unseen presence. And some sounds, to say the least, are music to the ears.

Knoxville is a musical town. Musicians come in all shapes and forms, and so comes the music. From rock to bluegrass to classical, the "Gateway to the Smokies" resounds with melody. Some musicians are quite conventional. Some... well...some are rather bizarre, to say the least. Some go beyond bizarre. Take, for example, the weird case of "Whistling Jack."

Whistling Jack is seen, as well as heard. Sometimes he appears as a distinct form, silhouetted by a streetlight. Other times he is a mere shadow flitting from the corner of the eye. However, by all accounts, his repertoire is severely limited.

He always is heard whistling a bright little tune. Most every-one recognizes it right away.... But I'm already getting ahead of my story.

Jack's life is as much of a mystery as his frequent appear-ances in one of the older parts of Knoxville. Sarah Temple-ton (not her real name) can tell you about Whistling Jack. She used to live on that street and heard him often, although she is reluctant to talk about it. "People around here think that I am crazy," she told me. "But I'm sure that they've heard Jack too. They're just afraid to admit it."

I had a hard time getting the story out of Sarah. I had heard about her from a mutual friend in Knoxville, and when he learned that I was writing a book about ghosts in the city, he arranged for the two of us to meet. "I'll tell you what I know," she said to me over lunch at Ruby Tuesday's on The Strip, "but I don't want my name to get around." I assured her that I would respect her privacy. (Actually her last name is so Rumanian that I doubt that I could spell it anyway!)

Sarah had heard about Jack from her father, who grew up in Knoxville during the Great Depression and, later, moved to Oak Ridge to work during World War II. "He told me that he had heard him lots of times," Sarah said. "He even saw him once or twice. At that time no one in the neighbor-hood was afraid of seeing Jack. There wasn't much money, and so there wasn't much to do except talk. He heard all kinds of stories about him, too.

"There was the story that Jack was once a postman who always whistled as he went about his route. Another story was that he was an old-time lamplighter. My father, himself, believed the one that Jack was a policeman who was killed on the street—right in front of our old house, in fact—by a drunk that he had tried to arrest."

Sarah was born in 1944, and when she was two years old, her family moved back to Knoxville. Her father had not sold the house, preferring to rent it out while he was in Oak Ridge. When he moved back in, nothing much had changed in the neighborhood. Even Jack was still there.

"One night, on my sixth birthday," Sarah began, "I was

awakened out of a sound sleep by someone whistling right outside my window. The house was a two-and-a-half story, white, Victorian structure, and my bedroom was on the second floor, in the front and facing the street. I got out of bed and went to the window. There, under an old-fashioned streetlight, I saw the figure of a man dressed in black. At least, I think he was dressed in black. He was in silhouette, so I couldn't see his face either.

"I didn't, of course, recognize him as a ghost. All I knew was that my sleep had been disturbed. I was groggy and a little grumpy. Also, at the time, I was kind of a forthright kid and said what was on my mind, much to the consternation of my parents. So I opened the window and yelled out for him to please stop making all that noise, and—I swear—he faded away right before my eyes!

"The next morning at breakfast, I told Daddy what had happened and he got a real funny look on his face. It was then that he told me about Whistling Jack and that I shouldn't be afraid of him. 'Ghosts can't hurt you,' he said, 'and Jack means no harm.'"

When Sarah learned who Jack really was, it made her a little nervous. Of course, she had heard all kinds of stories about ghosts which haunt houses and scare people to death. At six, her imagination was in full-blown maturity. But as time went on she forgot about Jack and was not as nervous about going into her room at night and turning off the lights. Then, a few years later, something happened to introduce her to the whistling ghost all over again.

"I remember that it was my twelfth birthday," Sarah said. "My parents had thrown a big party for me that day—it was on a Saturday—and had invited all my friends. By the time the last one had left at about nine that night, I was so tired that I could hardly see straight. So I thanked my parents for a wonderful birthday, bade them good night, and went up to my room.

"I had no sooner snuggled under the covers and closed my eyes when I heard this whistling outside my window. I looked over just in time to see a black shadow drift past. I jumped out of bed and rushed to the window. And there it was. This—it looked like a little black rain cloud—drifting down the street and this whistling was coming from it. And I swear, just as sure as we're sitting here, the tune he was whistling, just like when I was six years old, was 'Happy Birthday To You'!"

That was the last time that Sarah saw, or heard, Whistling Jack. Later she attended the University of Tennessee, and in her junior year, she got married and moved out of the old house.

"I've never been back there," she said as she was finishing her big salad. "I heard that all of the old houses look pretty bad right now and that the neighborhood is getting run-down. I have so many happy memories of the place that I think it would break my heart to see it again."

And what of Whistling Jack? Did he go back to the old neighborhood? Or did he even leave?

I really wanted to confirm Sarah's story about the ghost of Whistling Jack. I had heard a similar tale from several other people, but not from that neighborhood. After lunch, Sarah and I parted, and I drove out to her old street and asked around about Jack. Of course I was mostly met by blank stares. "I never heard about anything like that around here," one person told me. "But then, of course, I haven't lived here very long."

I was about ready to give up when I met a woman working at a convenience store. "I thought it was just my imagination," she said as she took my money for a package of molasses cookies. "I live on that very street, and one night a couple of months ago I heard whistling outside my window like you said. And I looked out and saw this man under a streetlight, all dark and shadowy. I got a little scared because we've been having some trouble around here with intruders. But as I watched him, he faded away. In a moment he was nowhere to be found.

"When I told my husband, he told me to go back to bed and let him sleep in peace. I never said any more about it. He thought I was bats."

"Let me ask you this," I said. "Was there any possibility that when you saw him it was your birthday?"

"Yeah," she answered. "And that's the funny thing about it. It sounded to me like the song he was whistling was 'Happy Birthday To You'!"

Forty years after its founding, Knoxville was known far and wide to be a wide-open town. There was a great perfusion of saloons, houses of ill repute, and other dens of iniquity that catered to the constant stream of visitors passing through the city.

The unbridled use of alcohol was an ever-present problem on the frontier. Early settlers were a lusty group who loved their whiskey. There was little entertainment on the frontier, so early pioneers had to make their own. Strong drink was always associated with good times. Unfortunately many people would rather drink than eat. Drunkenness was not only common, but, in some circles, a prerequisite of manhood. However, sometimes the party got out of hand.

Precious grain was needed for food for a growing population, not for the distilling of rotgut liquor. For example, before Tennessee became a state—and with the population of Davidson County expanding so rapidly, and farmland so hard to clear and cultivate in the wilderness—the Legislature of North Carolina passed "An Act to Prevent the Distillation of Spirituous Liquors for the Time Therein Mentioned in the County of Davidson."

Laws did little to curb drinking. The problem was that whiskey was cheap and plentiful. According to John Sevier's diary, a quart of brandy cost only one shilling and three pence. A whole gallon cost only five shillings! And two of Robertson County's main products were tobacco and whiskey.

Likewise, prostitution was widespread in early Knoxville. One house was run by a notorious madam with the unlikely nomenclature of Aunt Nellie Diddlemeyer. Aunt Nellie's ladies came from all sections of the frontier and, according to all accounts, were quite popular among the gentry. Not that they were "ladies" by any means. One nearly toothless lass, according to a customer, "smelt like my barnyard." However, what Aunt Nellie's girls lacked in social graces they more than made up for in athletic prowess. And every night men would assemble at Aunt Nellie's arena to enjoy her girls' performances. Legend has it that one of Aunt Nellie's charges was none other than "Big Nose" Kate, the future girlfriend of the notorious Doc Holliday, Georgia dentist, gambler, murderer, and bosom buddy of Wyatt Earp. Doc and the Earp brothers would later battle it out with the Clantons and McLowreys in the shoot-out at the OK Corral.

It would take many years before Knoxville became civilized. Our friend Parson Brownlow had much to do with that, but even that fiery temperance leader could not completely quell Knoxville's insatiable desire to party. And, as I said, sometimes things got out of hand. Here is an example:

People say that his name was Mac and that he died a violent death while sitting at his piano. One night there was a shattering of glass and he slumped forward on the keys, stone-cold dead even before the last notes he played had echoed through the room. Like the valiant frontiersman of old, Mac died ingloriously, but with his boots on. Now his ghost is said to carry on Mac's abbreviated career. The mystical strains of a Scott Joplin rag are sometimes heard drifting through that part of the old city where Mac once earned his dubious living. Mac was a pianist in a bordello.

Knoxville was at one time a dry city—a VERY dry city. Temperance leaders had the city firmly under control. In fact it has been only in the last few years that the juices of Bacchus have legally gurgled in public places within the municipal limits. Until that time, whiskey gushed illegally in various establishments that, in general, had a madam attached to them. The law usually turned a blind eye, and so, since these dens of iniquity served forbidden fruit (of all kinds) in such generous proportions, they did a booming business.

Mac was said to have been a frustrated concert pianist. His fingers, however, were short and stubby and not at all adapted to playing Rachmaninoff. So in order to make ends meet, Mac landed a job in one of the city's bordellos and pounded ragtime most every night.

Of course few ever listened to the music. The customers' minds were occupied with higher flights of fancy, so the muse didn't beckon them. Mac had a whiskey glass perched atop his rickety instrument for tips, but the bottom of the container was usually empty. Mac was paid fifty cents a night by the management, and that, basically, constituted his entire income. But Mac didn't really care. He had only himself to care for. Financially he was okay. Artistically, of course, he would much rather have been playing to SRO audiences at Carnegie Hall. The difference between Knoxville and New York was that most of Mac's listeners were not steady on their feet.

Poor Mac. He should have tended to his piano playing and left well enough alone, but he didn't. One night a surly inebriate decided to criticize Mac's expertise on the ivories. Legend has it that Mac was playing a Scott Joplin ditty called "Solitude," which is as sluggish a little tune as the title suggests. Most clients of the establishment wanted tunes as lively as their reverie. When the drunk suggested that Mac change from adagio to allegro, Mac told him where to stick his request, whereupon the drunk cracked the obstinate pianist over the head with a chunky beer mug.

When it was discovered that Mac had been dealt a death-blow, the management's first thought was to conceal the deed lest authorities intervene and close down the establishment. With the help of several patrons, Mac's flaccid body was dragged into a back room and covered with a dirty sheet. Fortunately for the killer, and everybody else concerned, Mac had no kin, so no one would miss him. Later that night the management tore up a few of the floorboards in the back room and buried the late musician beneath the sod.

The brothel, of course, is long gone. The building has long ago been swept up in the press of urban renewal that presently seizes downtown Knoxville. But the ghost of Mac is said to linger on.

The old building is now nothing more than an empty shell, but somewhere in that old structure, presumably, lie the bones of our unfortunate piano player. His spirit is restless. Late at night a passerby can still hear the tinkling of a ragtime piano drifting from somewhere within the brick and wood of the old structure. No one lives anywhere around there, so it couldn't be a phonograph playing. Nor is anyone likely to live there for some time to come.

The person who told me this story once said that he followed the music to a window. When he finally got up the courage to look through the broken glass, all he could see was darkness inside. But, he said, he continued to hear the music—just as clear as a bell.

"Why didn't you go inside?" I asked him.

He looked at me and then burst out laughing. I can't say that I blamed him very much. I wouldn't have gone in there either!

As I said, the building is now being renovated. Perhaps, in preparing to lay a new floor, some workman will discover a set of old bones buried in a forgotten back room. And maybe the discoverer will be a kindly soul who will give the bones a proper Christian burial. Some say that the lack of a Christian burial sometimes makes spirits restless and more apt to haunt. If that is true, perhaps that is just the thing that will silence Knoxville's ghostly piano player forever!

All the Inglorious Tricksters

How many readers of this book have ever "haunted" a house as a Halloween prank? How many have jumped out of a dark corner and yelled "Boo!"? Or who among us can truthfully say that we have never tried to scare a younger sibling half to death by saying that a ghost was lurking in a closet or under a bed? The truth of it is, all of us are tricksters and most do not need the excuse of Halloween to ply our trade. Reaction is the name of the game. Blame it on the dark side of our nature.

I remember one personal incident clearly. A young lady who spends a lot of time with our family was watching the movie *The Changeling* one lazy afternoon. Now, anyone who has ever seen this particular flick will remember that there are a couple of pretty good frights in it. To make a long story short, the young lady and I were munching on some dried apples as we watched this classic ghost tale unfold. I had seen the movie before, and at a particularly tense moment in the story, I tossed the plastic bag of apples across the room and it landed unexpectedly on her lap. She nearly had a heart attack!

"Have some more apples," I offered, immensely pleased with myself that I had caused her to jump halfway out of her skin. So, as you can see, even the most sophisticated and intelligent of us will turn into a ghastly trickster if the opportunity presents itself. Here's another incident offered as a case in point:

One day a Knoxville lad decided that he would give his buddies the scare of their lives. The first thing that he did was to spread the rumor that a certain old graveyard was haunted and that all a person had to do was to keep watch on a dark night and he would see a ghost. Many of his friends were hooked on the notion of a haunted graveyard, so it was only a matter of time until someone suggested that a group be dispatched to go out to investigate.

Before they met at the appointed hour—midnight to be exact—our trickster rigged up an old sheet to look like a ghost. Then he found a large tombstone that was directly beneath the overhanging limb of a tree. He tied a wire to the sheet, then strung the wire over the limb, reeled it out, and hid the end behind a convenient bush.

All was ready at the witching hour when his friends gathered at the graveyard, most of them absolutely convinced that they were going to see a spook. Of course, as there always is in such a crowd, there was a scoffer who said that he did not believe in the supernatural and if he ever saw a ghost, he would "spit in its eye."

Our trickster waited for a while, as suspense built among the assembled multitude. They whispered among themselves about dark and spooky nights, told ghost stories, and generally psyched up their imaginations. Finally, when he thought the time was right, the trickster slipped away from the crowd and sneaked over to his bush. He grabbed the end of the wire and yanked it with all of his might. Suddenly the "ghost" popped up from behind the tombstone, followed closely by terrified shouts and yells from the boys. Everyone took off running—including the scoffer who led the pack all the way back to town—while the trickster, immensely proud of his achievement, rolled around on the ground, laughing himself silly.

The trickster tale is as much a part of Knoxville folklore as the ghost story or monster tale. In fact, the trickster tale has been around for centuries. Take, for example, this ancient story attributed to the Greek slave, Aesop—"The Kid and the Wolf":

A Kid, returning without protection from the pasture, was pursued by a Wolf. Seeing he could not escape, he turned around, and said: "I know, friend Wolf, that I must be your prey, but before I die I would ask of you one favor. Play me a tune to which I may dance." The Wolf complied, and while he was piping and the Kid was dancing, some hounds hearing the sound ran up and began chasing the Wolf. Turning to the Kid, he said, "It is just what I deserve; for I, who am only a butcher, should not have turned piper to please you." MORAL: In time of dire need, clever thinking is key; or outwit your enemy to save your skin.

The Overmountain Cherokee Indians tell a similar story: One day a rat was walking through the forest when he came upon a huge blacksnake slinking through the underbrush. The snake wanted to eat the rat, who at the sudden sight of the reptile had backed up against a large rock. There was no way for the rat to escape, so he said to the snake, "Brother Snake, will you wait a moment before swallowing me while I pray to the gods of the forest to take my spirit?"

"Yes I will," the snake hissed. "But hurry up. I am very hungry."

The rat closed his eyes and appeared to be praying. But what the snake did not know was that the rat had seen an approaching buffalo that was, even now, bearing down on his enemy. The rat knew that buffaloes hated snakes and would kill one if they could. And he was right. The buffalo stomped down on the head of the snake and killed it. MORAL: In time of dire need, clever thinking is key; or outwit your enemy to save your skin. (Now where have we heard that before?)

Some stories, it seems, never change.

Sometimes a trickster's prank will trigger a chain of events that, over time, will evolve into a full-blown legend. I am convinced, for instance, that most "ghost light" stories began when someone played a trick on someone else.

Rory Fitzpatrick is a producer for Ulster Television and lives in Belfast, Ireland. About ten years ago he was a guest lecturer during one of the Scottish Studies summer programs at East Tennessee State University. One day Rory told me the story of a trick that became a legend. It was the story of "Happy Harry," an elderly man who most people in the neighborhood considered a bit daft.

"I remember that there were lights appearing along the

banks of a river," Rory began. "It was actually rather small—more of a creek. And I know the chap who was responsible for the whole thing and set it up. These 'ghost lights' were intended to frighten an old man who lived alone on a hill above the creek.

"Night after night this young fellow," Rory remembered, "walked along the banks of that creek in the dark with a lantern in his hand. And the old man would look out of his window. He'd turn away and look again, and the light would have disappeared. Actually the prankster had a large board which he periodically placed in front of the light so that it would appear to disappear.

"Well, some ten or fifteen years ago," Rory continued, "I was talking to some young people and the subject of ghosts came up. And they started to tell me the story of Happy Harry and the ghost light that haunted him. Now this was an example of a legend that began because someone had played a trick. I knew the truth about Happy Harry's ghost light, but I was not going to tell them and spoil their legend. Besides, I think they would have much more preferred the fiction than the truth."

Rory raises a point. Trickster pranks work simply because we want them to work. Psychologist Sharon Turnbull, who claims to be personally skeptical about the existence of ghosts, says, "All of us have a tendency, perhaps, toward self-delusion. Any of our senses, I think, can respond to things that are internally generated—for example, as in dreams or in the hallucinations of psychosis.... But how do you know if it's real? I think you can experience it, but how you document that, how you validate that through a shared experience, is going to be a very difficult problem."

The fundamental culture of Knoxville and of East Tennessee as well, as I have stated in this book, is Celtic and, as such, is highly conducive to belief in ghosts and acceptance of the supernatural. Therefore, stories of Knoxville tricksters are not limited merely to pranks by the living.

Several years ago a woman bought an antique inkwell from a little store in Jonesborough, brought it home, and placed it atop a 200-year-old writing desk. Immediately, strange things began to happen.

Each morning she would discover that the inkwell was moved from one side of the table to the other. At first she thought that her husband was rearranging the inkwell more to his liking and not telling his wife. But the woman's husband denied touching the artifact. Still she wondered whether he might be playing a prank on her. He had done this kind of thing before, and when his wife found it was a joke, her husband would respond with a very distinctive laugh—kind of a high-pitched "haw-haw."

About a week later, the husband unexpectedly died. After the funeral the woman, who was elderly, was sitting in the living room when she happened to glance over at the writing desk just in time to see the inkwell slowly move from one side of the highly polished wooden top to the other, without the benefit of human hands.

Then, from all around her, she heard a sound that she recognized immediately, and she knew that the mystery of the moving inkwell had been solved. A high-pitched "haw-haw" resounded through the room. Her husband had been moving the inkwell, and now he was returning from the grave to fess up to the prank.

After that, the inkwell never moved again.

Ghosts in graveyards are certainly a common motif in folklore. The infamous "Black Aggie" stories abound, and nearly every graveyard of any size has one. The most notorious is the "Black Angel" of Druid Ridge in Pikesville, Maryland.

The Black Angel was a small statue perched on top of a tombstone that marked the grave of newspaper publisher General Felix Angus, who died in 1923. According to local legend, the eyes of the Black Angel glow red at midnight, and this was duly reported in the local newspapers. And there was more: Anyone who looked at the Black Angel's glowing orbs would be struck blind, any pregnant woman who passed her would miscarry, and no grass would grow in the Angel's shadow.

One day in 1962, it was discovered that one of the Angel's

arms had been sawn off. The culprit was found with the arm, as well as the saw, in his possession. He was tried and found guilty of desecrating a sacred monument, even though he tried to explain that the Black Angel had done the sawing herself and had presented the arm to him.

The publicity turned the Black Angel monument into something of a tourist attraction. The Angus family was understandably unnerved at the fact that perfect strangers were gathered at the general's grave each night, waiting for ghostly happenings. Finally they had had enough. In 1967, the Black Angel was removed from the tombstone and presented to the Smithsonian Institution in Washington, D.C. Understandably, and at last word, it has not yet been put on display by that organization.

And the Black Aggie reported to lurk in the First Presbyterian graveyard is fairly well known. But there is one other case that I have been able to unearth, not in Knoxville, but nearby in Knox County.

In the early days of settlement of East Tennessee, community graveyards like the one at First Presbyterian Church were rare. Rather, small private family graveyards were established on each farm. Generations of family members were buried there. If the family owned slaves, it was customary to bury them there, too, in a section all to themselves. There was segregation even in death.

Family plots were usually located on top of a hill, presumably to be closest to the Resurrection when, according to the Bible, the dead would be the first called. And these cemeteries, like larger ones, always faced east, toward the rising sun—the lustrous symbol of the Resurrection.

While families continued to own their farms, the graveyards were kept in good repair, were swept free of brush, and their grass was neatly manicured. Graves that sunk due to rotting wooden coffins—a common occurrence before concrete burial vaults—were promptly filled in, as were the tunnels of burrowing animals. But if the family sold their land, or as in many cases during the Great Depression, their farms were repossessed, the old graveyards were sometimes forgotten and would become overgrown and run-down.

One of these family graveyards is located between Knoxville and Maryville in a little clump of trees about a quarter mile off State Route 129. The original land was part of a grant from the state of North Carolina, before the Southwest Territory was ceded to the United States, and belonged to a man named Wadell (or Wadel). The land was in the family for years, and generations of Wadells were buried in the old family plot.

The last Wadell died without an heir, and as the story goes, the farm passed to the family of his wife, who promptly sold it for a good profit. The family graveyard, of course, fell into ruin, and precious little of it can still be seen today—only a few markers lie hidden in the underbrush. But, apparently, the ghost of old man Wadell still roams among the tombstones and scrub, perhaps angry that the old homestead was sold.

The ghost is seen as a white mist, hovering several feet above the ground. Sometimes it floats from one side of the graveyard to the other. Sometimes it remains stationary. At any rate the legend, as well as the ghost, has been a magnet for thrill seekers for years. Since the area is rather remote, few intruders have been caught and prosecuted for trespassing, even though the land is well-posted. And, perhaps, that is one of the major reasons that the curious are drawn to old graveyards that are rumored to be haunted—the imagined danger of something supernatural and unexplained, and the very real danger of getting caught by irate landowners who do not appreciate uninvited visitors who intrude on their property.

One can only wonder what the ghosts think of the intrusion!

Bibliography
BOOKS

Allison, John. *Dropped Stitches in Tennessee History* (1897). Nashville/Charles Elder, 1971.

Brewer, Alberta and Carson. *Valley So Wild: A Folk History.* Knoxville/East Tennessee Historical Society, 1975.

Buchanan, Lamont. *A Pictorial History of the Confederacy.* New York/Bonanza Books, 1951.

Creekmore, Betsey Beeler. *Knoxville* (Second Edition) Knoxville/University of Tennessee Press, 1967.

Donaldson, Gordon. *The Scot Overseas.* Westport/Greenwood Press, 1976.

Dykeman, Wilma. *The French Broad.* Knoxville/University of Tennessee Press, 1955.

Folmsbee, Stanley J., Robert E. Corlew, Enoch L. Mitchell. *Tennessee: A Short History.* Knoxville/University of Tennessee Press, 1969.

Foote, Shelby. *The War Between the States A Narrative: Fort Sumter to Perryville.* New York/Vintage Books, 1986.

——————— *The War Between the States A Narrative: Fredericksburg to Meridian,* New York/Vintage Books, 1986

Foster, Austin P. *Counties of Tennessee.* Nashville/Tennessee Department of Education, 1923.

Garrett, William Robertson and Albert Virgil Goodpasture. *History of Tennessee: Its People and Its Institutions.* Nashville/Brandon Printing Co., 1900.

Gerson, Noel B. *Franklin: America's Lost State.* New York/Crowell-Collier Press, 1968.

_____*Goodspeed's History of Tennessee.* Nashville/Goodspeed Publishers, 1887.

Hardin, Terri (Editor). *Legends and Lore of the American Indians.* New York/Barnes and Noble, 1993.

Judd, Cameron. *The Bridge Burners.* Johnson City/The Overmountain Press, 1996.

Kennedy, Billy. *The Scots-Irish in the Hills of Tennessee.* Londonderry/Causeway Press, 1995.

Long, E.B. and Barbara Long. *The War Between the States Day by Day: An Almanac 1961-1965.* Garden City/Doubleday, 1971.

McDonald, Michael J. and William Bruce Wheeler. *Knoxville, Tennessee: Continuity and Change In An Appalachian City.* Knoxville/University of Tennessee Press, 1990.

Moore, John Trotwood and Austin P. Foster. *Tennessee: The Volunteer State 1769-1923.* Two Volumes. Nashville/S. J. Clarke Publishing Company, 1923.

Montgomery, James Riley, Stanley J. Folmsbee, and Lee Seifert Greene. *To Foster Knowledge: A History of The University of Tennessee 1794-1970.* Knoxville/University of Tennessee Press, 1984.

Pine, L.G. *The Highland Clans.* Rutland/Charles E. Tuttle, Inc. 1972.

Ramsey, J.G.M. *The Annals of Tennessee to the End of the Eighteenth Century.* Charleston/Walker and James, 1853.

Smith, J. Gray. *Historical, Statistical, and Descriptive Review of East Tennessee* (1842). Spartanburg/The Reprint Company, 1974.

Starkey, Marion L. *The Cherokee Nation.* North Dighton, Mass./JG Press, 1973.

Temple, Oliver P. *East Tennessee and the War Between the States* (1899) Reprint. Johnson City/The Overmountain Press, 1995.

Tennessee Historical Commission/Tennessee Historical Society. *Tennessee Old and New (1796-1946).* Two Volumes. Kingsport/Kingsport Press, 1946.

Tennessee Historical Society. *The Tennessee Encyclopedia of History and Culture.* Carroll Van West, Editor-In-Chief. Nashville/Rutledge Hill Press, 1998.

Wilson, Charles Reagan and William Ferris, Editors. *Encyclopedia of Southern Culture.* Wilmington/University of North Carolina Press, 1989.

ARTICLES

Fisher, Noel. "Definitions of Loyalty: Attitudes and Expectations of the Civil War in East Tennessee." Knoxville/*The Journal of East Tennessee History.* No. 67, 1995.

Garber, Anna. "Ghosts From The Bijou's Past Wander The Old Theater Still" *The Knoxville Journal,* October 31, 1989.

Loveday, Yvonne. "Who Was Sophie? Knoxville/*Torch-bearer*. University of Tennessee, Fall 1998.

Loveday, Yvonne. "Historically Haunted Locations Provide Shocking Ghost Stories" *Knoxville News-Sentinel*, October 30, 1991.

McRary, Amy. "Who-o-o's At Home In Those Historic Houses?" *Knoxville News-Sentinel*. October 31, 1995.

McRary, Amy. "Haunted Knoxville" *Knoxville News-Sentinel*, October 16, 1998.

Neeley, Jack. "The Beast of Middlebrook" *Knoxville Metropulse*. October 30-November 6, 1994.

Neeley, Jack. "Not So Tall Tales: Truth can be stranger than fiction—especially when it comes to Knoxville's urban legends">http://www.metropulse.com/dir_zine/dir_1999/9 03/t_cover.html< Knoxville/Metropulse Online. Retrieved March 3, 1999.

Thomas, John Kyle. "The Cultural Reconstruction of an Appalachian City: Knoxville, Tennessee, and the Coming of the Movies. Knoxville/*The Journal of East Tennessee History*, No. 65, 1993.

Turczyn, Coury. "Cinema Stars: Knoxville's last two surviving jewels from the golden age of moviegoing find a new lease on life.">http://www.metropulse.com/dir_zine/dir_ 1998/842/t_cover.html< Knoxville/Metropulse Online. Retrieved March 2, 1999.

WEBSITES

———— "Government in Knoxville." Retrieved April 14, 1999.>http://www.knoxvilletennessee.com/government. html<

Martin, Ken. "History of the Cherokee" >http: //afsnet.org/< Retrieved April 1, 1999.

———— Knoxville News-Sentinel >http://www. knoxnews.com/< Homepage

———— "Tennessee Theatre, The" >http://tennessee theatre.com/< Knoxville/Homepage.

———— "University of Tennessee, Knoxville" >http: //www.utk.edu/< Homepage.